VENTURA COUNTY
LIMA BEANS

VENTURA COUNTY
LIMA BEANS
· A HISTORY ·

JEFFREY WAYNE MAULHARDT

AMERICAN PALATE

Published by American Palate
A Division of The History Press
Charleston, SC
www.historypress.com

Front cover, top, left to right: The ladies at the bean warehouse in Camarillo sorting lima beans looking for damaged beans. Ramon Feliz supervising. *Pleasant Valley Historical Society*; Harold Gill in the "doghouse" sewing lima bean sacks circa 1940s. *Jim Gill*; John McGrath on his Allis Chalmers tractor weeding between the rows of Fordhook lima beans on his Patterson Ranch property. *Tim McGrath*; *bottom*: A lima bean ranch near Ventura, California, circa 1910. The creator of the postcard image was J.R. Brakey. *Evangeline Maulhardt-Hopson.*
Back cover, top: Louis Maulhardt threshing outfit collecting discarded chaff from threshed beans near Camarillo Heights, circa 1910. *Reid and Florence Hornbeck*; *inset*: A two-pound bag for Ventura County–grown lima beans sold at the Oxnard Historic Farm Park. *Jeff Maulhardt.*

First published 2024

Manufactured in the United States

ISBN 9781467157049

Library of Congress Control Number: 2024937020

CONTENTS

ACKNOWLEDGEMENTS

The genesis of the book came about with a conversation with Mike Naumann, descendant of a longtime agricultural family of the Oxnard Plain, the Samuel Naumann family. Mike provided the lima beans for the 150th anniversary of Ventura County at the Oxnard Historic Farm Park, where I am the director and founder. The positive response to the beans that afternoon led me to approach Mike about doing a follow-up annual event, a Lima Bean Fest. The wheels started turning, and I approached Arcadia for the twelfth time and here we are. So my initial thanks go out to Mike, who invited me out when he was threshing beans a few weeks later. Mike has also provided some invaluable connections in the lima bean world as well as access to his extensive lima bean images and articles.

A big thanks also goes to his cousin Frank Naumann, who has been there for me from the beginning of my book publishing, as you'll see a reference to his contributions in most of my seventeen local history books. Frank took a series of pictures from 1991 to 1993 of the few remaining lima bean threshers. Out of these 350 color slides, many serve as the inspiration for the color images in this book.

One of Mike's introductions was to Tom Schott, whose family was in the Fordhook lima bean business for three generations. Tom gave me an education on the growing and harvesting of the green limas, and he's now part of my Lima Bean Family.

Paul DeBusschere was also instrumental in helping me fill in the gaps about the more recent lima bean history.

- James Reiman has been supportive of the Oxnard Historic Farm Park as well as this venture.

Someone who was instrumental in supporting my history endeavors at the Farm Park and my publication is someone who is no longer with us but deserves a shout-out, Chuck Covarrubias. Chuck's California roots date back to 1834, when his ancestor Jose Maria Covarrubias came with the Hijar-Padres party. Chuck was instrumental in helping me collect agricultural artifacts over the years, including our two vintage bean threshers built by the Ventura Implement and Manufacturing company. Chuck brought in other farming enthusiasts and financial supporters including the late, great Jim Gill, Bill Lenox and Joe Pena. They all contributed to the lima bean legacy. Following in his footsteps is his son David Covarrubias, who has picked up where Chuck left off.

Thank you to Korinne Bell, from the Ventura County Agricultural Commission office, for opening the door to the office, and thank you to Melonie Morgan for providing me with decades worth of crop reports.

Thanks also to Francis Giudici, president of LA Hearne Co. in Kings City, where the lima beans from California are cleaned and sold. It was to my great surprise to learn upon my introductory email that Francis not only knew my uncle and godfather, Bob Maulhardt Jr., but Uncle Bob was his mentor and friend as well. Small world. From there, the door was open to the information I needed from Francis and his expertise.

Thank you to Craig Held for his lima bean archives and for his Santa Paula input, pictures and connecting me to other images from both Paul Ayers and Carlos Juarez from the Santa Paula Historical Society. Also thank you to Alison Ayers O'Neill for sharing a Falkner ranch image.

Bill Lenox and Joe Pena were instrumental in helping me identify the various threshers and tractors as well as sharing their knowledge of the lima bean industry.

The ladies from Pleasant Valley Historical Society, Beth Miller and Joy Todd, came through big time. In addition to the three Bill Milligan panoramic pictures he donated to the society, the organization provided me with several images of the lady bean sorters in Camarillo as well several other useful images.

Thanks to Card Lady descendants John Dullam, Marcia Hopper Smith and Andy Hooper for coordinating the use of the Oxnard Frozen Foods board members picture.

Also, another set of Card Lady relatives, Paul Thomas and his brothers Frank, David, Jim, John and Jed deserve a shout-out for sending me over one hundred images of their dad, Art Thomas, threshing beans on the Oxnard Plain and their ranch in Oregon. Their mother, Sue, was always good for a bowl of lima beans whether they were wanted or not.

Thanks to Jayme Yahr from the Carpinteria Valley Historical Society and Hanna Rogers from the Museum of Ventura County for their efforts in getting me the images requested for this publication.

I appreciate the prompt and helpful correspondences with the Arcadia representative, Laurie Krill.

I'd like to acknowledge the support of Kasey Calcagno for sponsoring my lima bean meetings at Spanish Hills Club and for putting the lima bean hummus on the menu.

As the reintroduction of lima beans to the county has already been planted with the preparation of this book and establishment of the annual Lima Bean Fest, the harvest is starting to show up on menus for several local restaurants whose recipes are included in the recipe chapter. To accommodate the many stories, images and information that will follow with this publication, I expect to gather enough info for a series of self-published books to coincide with each of the annual Lima Bean Fest events at the Oxnard Historic Farm Park.

Finally, I want to thank my wife, Deb, for putting lima beans back on the table. She has come up with a recipe that is so tasty I had to include it in this publication.

INTRODUCTION

You either hated them or loved them! Lima beans were still a big part of our lives while growing up in Ventura County in the 1960s and '70s. There were still lima bean fields, and in the fall, there were bean threshers working through the night. And there were lima beans on the plate.

To me, lima beans were filling. As a youngster active in sports, I was always ready for the next meal. When visiting certain farming families, you could count on a pot of beans on the stove. Some recipes included limas in the chili. This was much more palatable for those reluctant lima bean eaters. Then there were the casseroles that included limas. Those too, could sway those on the fence. Others knew lima beans as part of a succotash dish. Again, for me, I was all-in.

Also, anyone who grew up in the area and was associated with any farming family knew of the May gray and June gloom, but we all called it lima bean weather. The fog served as the irrigation for the beans. A rare summer rain or early fall downpour were dreaded events, spoiling the beans' ability to maximize their growth and begin to dry out.

One of fun things associated with lima beans was the bean thresher. It sat dormant for ten months, and the two-story machine was transformed in a boy's imagination into a ship with the metal climbing stairs and the top deck with the lookout station.

Another experience I had with lima beans came during a high school summer when my dad secured me a lima bean field on the corner of Hueneme Road and Saviers. It was my job for one month to walk between the limas and hoe out the strangling morning glory plant that reduced the vitality of the bean plant. Talk about long, boring and school-inspiring—try that for a summer.

Later in life after I established a career as a teacher, I had a house in Camarillo with almost two acres of land. Every house I'd lived in up to this time included an avocado tree that I planted. But with this property, I could plant a dozen trees and still have room for more plantings. I decided to grow some lima beans, and I contacted a local farmer, Emil Pfeiler Jr., and he gave me some "King of the garden" lima beans. After planting several long rows of beans, I returned to Mr. Pfeiler and asked him how many times I should water the beans. He told me to water the plants two or three times. I asked, "Per week?" And he incredulously replied, "No, for the summer!" So I learned the value of dry farming.

Another thing we heard while growing up in Ventura County in the 1960s was that we were the Lima Bean Capital of the World. At times, Oxnard claimed the title, as did Camarillo. However, there was no denying the importance of the lima bean to the development of the county. Several communities contributed to the lima bean claim, including Santa Paula, Saticoy, Montalvo and Ventura.

The bean's importance to the county dates back to 1893 when the county built a pagoda structure loaded with two thousand pounds of lima beans at the Chicago World's Fair. The Ventura County Courthouse building, now City Hall, was completed in 1913 and included fifteen lima bean bouquets as part of the façade. The government seized the county's crop in 1917 to feed the troops fighting World War I. The county sent lima beans to several presidents over the years. The county even lobbied for and was granted a National Lima Bean Week in 1941.

I found it interesting to learn that lima beans were used as a substitute for meat during the two world wars as well as during the Great Depression. Finding a recipe for poverty stew was a revelation.

The development of the frozen food industry in the 1940s gave the beans a new life. No longer were the cooks of the kitchen having to soak their beans overnight before getting lima beans on the table. Stokely Van Camp and Ventura Farms Frozen Foods were on the front line of innovation in packaging and distributing the Fordhook lima beans.

And finally, I found out that lima beans aren't dead. Dry limas are still grown in California and, more specifically, the Oxnard Plain. I learned that the beans are now considered a superfood, rich with protein, fiber, iron, antioxidants, zinc, potassium and more. This all made me hungry for more history on the lima bean.

It's been written and talked about for years. We were the Lima Bean Capital of the World! Here's the story.

1
A SHIP FROM LIMA

There are many stories on the origin of the lima bean (*Phaseolus lunatus* L.) as well as the lima bean industry. W.W. Mackie, an agronomist at the University of California, Berkley, wrote an article in the journal *Hillgardia* in the 1940s and said that the large limas came from the Amazon Valley and the small varieties have been found in the West Indies and Central America. He reported that there were ninety-six varieties of lima beans from which there are three branches of the family: Hopi, which extended north the United States; Carib, carried to the West Indies and Amazon basin; and Inca, which traveled south to Peru. The all belong to a single species. However, more recent scholarship indicates the existence of only two gene pools, labeled Mesoamerican and Andean.

Research has shown that Columbus found lima beans in Cuba, and beans were also discovered in Virginia, south of the Potomac River. Even George Washington was aware of the beans according to a letter he wrote to his gardener.

The origin of the development of the lima bean industry also has some challenges. Charles Outland, a local historian and author and editor, compiled several notebooks of historical references from early newspapers and created an index of historical topics. Commenting on a September 20, 1907 reference in the *Ventura Free Press* on the first plantings of lima beans, Outland noted: "If all the claimants to raising the first limas were laid end to end they would reach across California. Fr. Serra in one of his letters requesting supplies from Mexico requested lima beans, undoubtedly to be used as seed in the Mission gardens. Until someone comes up with an earlier claim, the compiler of this notebook will string along with the good padre."

While the missions may have planted lima beans in their gardens in the eighteenth century, the bean was certainly not planted commercially.

The seed was advertised by H. McNally Company in the Northern California newspaper *Daily Alta California* as early as 1855. In 1859, an article appeared in the magazine *California Culturist* in which the author encouraged the planting of lima beans for vegetable gardens.

Though the bean is native to Guatemala, it was at the port of Callao, Peru, and from its surrounding hillsides near Lima that the plant thrived. Ships often loaded their galleys with a variety of food samples for the crew as well as for trading.

Carpinteria, like most of Southern California in the 1860s, was devoid of farming. The southern section of California was sparsely populated. The cattle industry started by the early Californios was a drought away from disappearing and the years 1863 and 1864 proved to be the nail in the coffin for original landowners. As miners from Northern California made their way down the state to look for a new way to strike gold, Santa Barbara County looked to have some potential for agriculture.

One of the more substantial clues to who planted the first commercial crop of lima beans goes back to the 1907 article that Outland referenced. The article quotes William Leachman Lewis, the oldest son of Henry Lewis from Carpenteria, who claimed that his father planted the beans as early as 1868 after receiving the bean from another farmer, Robert McAllister.

Another article in the *California Cultivator* magazine published in December 1915 supports this claim. Joseph Lewis, a second son of Henry Lewis, stated that Robert McAlister visited a vessel anchored of the coast of Santa Barbara in 1868 and was invited to a meal. McAlister "begged for a hatful of beans for trying out under the California conditions, afterward dividing them with Mr. Henry Lewis."[1] While others have stated that Henry Lewis himself was the one to visit the ship, it seems that his two sons would have made that claim. Therefore, the McAllister reference holds up, and the fact that he shared the beans still puts them in Lewis hands. Therefore, they most likely both planted the seeds.

Henry Lewis arrived in Carpinteria in the spring of 1862. He was born in 1830 in Prince Williams County, Virginia. By 1857, he had come to Northern California with his wife, Elizabeth Chattin, and headed toward the mines in Tuolumne County. As his grandson Guy E. Lewis wrote years later, "After six months experience he came out with rheumatism and little else."[2] This led to his move to Half Moon Bay, where he farmed for three years before he traveled one last time to the mesa of Carpinteria, where he purchased eighty acres.

After clearing the land of sagebrush, Lewis planted corn without the aid of irrigation. By 1868, his neighbor Robert McAllister had come in contact with the lima beans, and Lewis began experimenting with the plants. Henry Lewis planted his on the hillsides of his ranch, and they flourished.[3] Lewis continued raising lima beans and experimenting with different improvements through selection, trial and error. The early crops produced a long vine, but Lewis noticed that there were a few plants that were different than the rest. While having shorter vines, the plant contained just as many if not more pods. The plant would produce pods more around the root of the vine, called the crown set. Henry had his third son, Dozier, collect these stray plants until he had enough seed to plant his entire crop of these preferred beans. These became known as the Lewis Lima. These beans soon produced forty 80-pound sacks per acre or 3,200 pounds per acre.[4] They became the favored limas for many years.

Henry Lewis, along with Robert McAllister, planted the first lima beans in Carpinteria, and he developed the Lewis Lima bean variety through selection. Three of his sons—William, Joseph and Dozier Lewis—helped develop the lima bean industry in Ventura County. *Jeff Maulhardt.*

Robert McAllister was from Ireland and came to Northern California in search of gold. Like many miners, he found gold in other parts of the state. He purchased fifty-three acres in Carpenteria, and by 1868 he had tried planting the lima beans he received in his garden. The soil and climate proved friendly to the bean plant. The vine plan thrived, despite not being staked up or having established irrigation.

Within a few years, word on the success of the bean was spreading. On October 8, 1870, the *Santa Barbara Weekly* announced that one of the most successful farmers on the county claimed the lima bean was the most profitable bean to raise. The lima bean cost one cent per pound, and growers could make two and a half cents per pound. Unfortunately, the paper did

VENTURA COUNTY LIMA BEANS

Robert McAllister obtained a quantity of lima beans from a ship from Lima, Peru, that anchored off the coast of Santa Barbara. The seed originated from Guatemala and thrived in the hills of Peru. By the 1870s, lima beans in Carpinteria were a prolific crop. *Jeff Maulhardt.*

not give the name of the farmer, though both Lewis and McAllister were farming in the area at this time.

Colonel Russell Heath, who settled in Carpenteria in 1858, lived next to the McAllister ranch. He planted a vineyard of ten thousand vines and a nursery of almonds as well as an extensive orchard of walnuts. He became the first sheriff of Santa Barbara County and later a district attorney and assemblyman.

Other early settlers included Steven and Sarah Olmstead, E.S. Lowery, John Nidever, Thomas Callis, William Callis, Andrew Bailard, Lawrence Bailard, John Pyster, Thomas Cravens, John Walker, William Benn, Henry Fish, George Doubleday, E.J. Knapp, the Taylor family and O.N. Caldwell.

Incoming settlers joined the already established families, who owned between ten and sixty acres, including Rafael Ayala, Juan and Carlos Rodriguez, Jose and Carlos Ruiz, Gabriel Hernandez, Jose Cota, Jose Antonia Ruiz, Juan Carrillo, Elberto Espinoza, Hilario Ornalez and the families of Pico, Domingo, Valencias and Sanchez.

The *Santa Barbara Press* reported that Captain Jonathon Mayhew planted one hundred acres of lima beans in May 1871. Mayhew lived at the Light

18

House on the mesa a few miles south of the town of Santa Barbara. However, he planted the beans thirty-five miles south on this property in the Santa Clara Valley near the Santa Clara River, closer to the Ventura area.

Robert McAlister planted nine acres in 1872 that produced eleven tons of beans. One vine of pods weighed four pounds. He was able to sell them for five cents a pound.[5] Unfortunately, McAllister didn't witness the growth of the bean's popularity, as he died in March 1874 at the age of forty-four at the home of his neighbor, Russell Heath.

A.J. Williams also experimented with the seed and readily shared with the *Morning Press* newspaper as reported on December 11, 1873. D.L. Clark also shared a basket of lima beans that ended up being reported in the newspaper.

Henry Fish arrived in Carpinteria from New York in 1873. He met up with Robert McAllister and received a quantity of beans. Fish became intrigued with the lima bean and the facts that they did not need to be poled up and the vines did not mold or mildew while lying on the soil. And because there was no frost until later in the year, the beans had plenty of time to mature.

Robert Fish next decided to contact D.M. Ferry & Co. from Detroit, Michigan, which sold garden seeds. He wrote a letter explaining the benefits of selling lima beans, and after a short visit, Henry Fish began a many-

Henry Fish standing among his Fordhook beans, in front of his house in Carpinteria, circa 1910. *Carpinteria Valley Historical Society.*

decades-long relationship with the seed distributor. This led him to establish the Henry Fish Seed Company in 1876. Over the years, Fish and his son Berrien produced over twenty varieties of lima beans.

By 1888, Fish was sending thirty thousand pounds of bean seeds to Ferry. Fish also began selling the seeds to other the East Coast companies. His son Henry Berrien Fish continued to search for new varieties of lima beans among their plantings. In 1903, Berrien found a plant that was different than the others. He took good care of the plant and saved every seed from its initial discovery year. The plant was similar in appearance to the Challenger lima bean but grew in a bush form, like the Dreer's bush variety. The pods and the beans were much larger. It took several plantings in the coming years to have enough plants to put the bean to the taste test. The beans had an almost "nutty" flavor and eventually earned the nickname "Butter Bean." Producers would soon find out that the bean retained its flavor whether canned, blanched or frozen.

Henry Fish sent the seeds to several seed companies to plant for themselves in hopes they would take on the sale of the seeds. In 1906, Atlee Burpee, from Burpee Seed Company, paid top dollar for the rights to name the new lima bean and chose Fordhook, after his test garden at Doylestown, Pennsylvania, and by 1907, the Fordhook lima bean had been introduced to the public.

Santa Barbara built Stearns Wharf in 1872, but the lima bean growers needed a wharf closer to home. Frank Smith was a wharfinger, or manager, of Stearns Wharf. He had an office at Stearns Wharf at the Agent Marine Department. Frank and his brother Nelson Smith opened a lumberyard in Carpenteria in 1874. Along with their brother Milton, the Smiths built a four-hundred-foot wharf referred to as Smith's Wharf. By December 1874, six thousand sacks of beans had been shipped from the Smith brothers' wharf. Within a few years, they added another four hundred feet. The Smith brothers owned eleven acres connecting their wharf. Their older brother Milton named the area Serena for its tranquil setting. The wharf was later rechristened Serena Wharf. The wharf lasted until 1911, when ears of crashing waves took their toll and closed the pier. Attempts to rebuild the wharf over the next several years failed to materialize.

Many were trying their hand at growing the new crop. A Mr. Sutton was reported to be using one of the first bean harvesters in 1874. Steven Olmstead would also be using a thresher within a short time. He would average close to 1,800 pounds per acre.

The Fordhook lima bean was developed by Henry Fish in Carpinteria. Fish sold the patent to Altee Burpee, who named it after his farm in Pennsylvania. *Jeff Maulhardt.*

Just north of Carpenteria in Goleta, lima beans were being introduced. A man by the name of Herrick, manager of the Patterson ranch in Goleta, planted eight acres of lima beans in 1875. The local paper made note of the impressive harvest and wondered why more farmers weren't planting the bean: "The fame of the Lima beans of this vicinity for size and flavor has long been established, and we wonder that the crop is not more generally cultivated."[6]

Back in Carpenteria, Andrew Bailard planted sixteen acres of lima beans in 1875 that yielded 48,800 pounds. In 1878, it was reported that five thousand sacks of lima beans were shipped from the Carpinteria Wharf.

In January 1880, the local paper reported that there would be one thousand acres of lima beans sown in Carpenteria.[7] Henry Lewis planted sixty-five acres that produced 1,265 sacks weighing 121,830 pounds. Lewis planted fifty acres in 1883 that produced a ton an acre.

One of the biggest bean growers in these early years was the Bailard ranch. Andrew and Martha Bailard came from Baden, Germany. Like

Bean harvesting on the Martin Ranch, Carpenteria, circa 1905. The Martin family arrived in Carpinteria in 1870. *Carpinteria Valley Historical Society.*

Bean harvesting on James Washington Ogan Ranch, Carpinteria, circa 1915. The Ogan family arrived in Carpinteria in 1870. *Carpinteria Valley Historical Society.*

Henry Lewis, the Bailards spent time in Half Moon Bay before traveling south to Carpenteria. Andrew purchased 500 acres. He died in 1876, and his sons William and John Bailard took over. On 16 acres, they raised 24,000 pounds of beans. George Doubleday raised 2,500 pounds of limas per acre on his 50-acre ranch. On a 120-acre ranch, E.J. Knapp grew 49 acres of beans that produced 83,000 pounds.

Lompoc in Santa Barbara County was another area of developing lima bean production. As early as 1886, farmers were producing three thousand pounds per acre.

In the meantime, Henry Lewis's son Joseph Francis Lewis perfected a strand that he marketed in Ventura County with Frank Barnard as the Lewis Common Lima. He rented 260 acres near Camarillo in 1889. The following year, he leased 300 acres in Montalvo for a ten-year period before returning to Camarillo in 1901 to plant a large portion of the Adolfo Camarillo ranch in lima beans. By 1906, Joseph Lewis had purchased over 8,000 acres, which he continued to farm for the next several decades.

Joseph Lewis also improved the industry by adapting a grain thresher to separate the pod from the vine and added a "sacker" on the thresher to improve efficiency. He also put wheels on the bean cultivator and attached knives to a sled for cutting the beans.

Carpenteria sent not only lima beans to Ventura County but also many families who continued farming and introducing the crop to the area. Among the families that moved to Ventura County were the sons of Henry Lewis: William Leachman Lewis, Joseph Lewis and Dozier Lewis. Richardson brothers, John Benn and the Mayhew, Everett, Vance and Ward families also relocated to the more expansive Ventura County.

2

FROM BARLEY TO LIMAS

I n the 1850s, Ventura County was made up of sparsely populated ranchos and survived through hospitality, trade and contributions provided by the Native people. Agriculture was still a personal endeavor in the area. The cattle industry lived and died with the varying levels of precipitation; the final blow came during the drought years of 1863–64, when nearly fifteen thousand head of cattle perished due to a lack of grasslands to feed on. Many of the original land grantees were forced to sell the land they originally retained when California joined the Union in 1850. Squatters began looking for government land to homestead.

The year 1867 was a turning point in the development of agriculture in Ventura County. Two ranchos, El Rio de Santa Clara o la Colonia, containing over forty-four thousand acres, and Santa Paula y Saticoy Rancho, over sixty-two thousand acres, began to be portioned off into farmland. This brought in people from the east as well as former miners from the north to start a new life in the barren ranchos. Thomas Scott, a railroad executive and oil investor from Pennsylvania, purchased the majority of the Colonia Rancho in 1864 along with portions of several other Ventura County ranchos for the purpose of developing a West Coast oil industry. George G. Briggs purchased the entire Santa Paula Y Saticoy Rancho in 1862 with the idea of planting fruit trees that would bear fruit before the Northern California market. Neither man was able to achieve his original goal, but a whole new market opened up with the breakup of the ranchos into parcels for sale for farming.

The motivation for Scott to purchase Southern California ranchos—including Ranchos of Ojai, Las Posas, Simi and Colonia (Oxnard)—came after he became aware of a report by Benjamin Silliman after his visit to Ojai and Ventura area in 1864 in which he witnessed "rivers" of oil. However, reaching the buried reserves proved frustrating to several supervisors such as Thomas Bard, who arrived to Ojai from Pennsylvania in 1865. After nearly two years of little progress in drilling for the big payday, Bard was ready to return to Pennsylvania and even sent a rider to Los Angeles with a telegram of his resignation on December 8, 1866, to take effect on January 10, 1867. However, Scott did not acknowledge Bard's letter, and Bard was obligated to continue with his oil duties.

The Colonia Rancho was officially granted to eight soldiers from Santa Barbara. Scott was unable to purchase the portion owned by Rafael Gonzalez. Gonzalez sold his portions to Juan Camarillo and Jose Lobero. Lobero sold one thousand acres to Borchard, and Camarillo would lease then sell to the Maulhardt family.

The original land grant of Santa Paula y Saticoy was awarded to Manuel Jimeno Casarin in 1840 and confirmed in 1843 and contained 17,773 acres.

Gonzales Ranch off Gonzales Road, Oxnard, part of the original Colonia grant. While original grantee Rafael Gonzalez returned to his adobe home in Santa Barbara in the 1860s, several of his children retained small tracts of land. Ed Gonzales, a grandson, grew fifteen acres of lima beans as early as 1891. *Chuck Covarrubias.*

Casarin served as secretary of state to Governors Alvarado and Micheltorena. Casarin married the daughter of Jose de la Guerra y Noriega, and he owned Rancho Salsipuedes Rancho in Santa Cruz County and Rancho Jimeno in Yolo County. Casarin did not live on his Southern California rancho, and by 1852 he had sold the land to Levi Parsons, Eugene Casserly, J.B. Crocket, David Mahoney and others. The name J.P. Davison is also connected to the sale.[8] Soon, these men sold the rancho to the More brothers, Thomas, Andrew and Henry.

By 1862, the More brothers had sold the rancho to George G. Briggs from Marysville. Briggs came to California from New York seeking gold but turned his interests toward growing fruit. In 1850, he began planting orchards and nurseries at the river bottom of the Yuba River near Marysville. In 1851, he grew 25 acres of watermelons and made $17,000.[9] He planted 58,000 trees along the Yuba River as well as on the shores of the Feather and Sacramento Rivers. He was doing well, grossing $100,000 by 1859.[10] Unfortunately, the biblical rains in Northern California in 1862 wiped out his 58,000 fruit trees. He took his previous profits and purchased the 17,773-acre rancho for $45,000.[11] In addition to planting another fruit orchard with the hopes that his fruit would bear earlier than the northern markets, Briggs was looking to create a colony.

Briggs chose a spot more inland to plant his orchards in Santa Paula so as not to be disappointed if the Santa Clara River repeated the disastrous flooding he experienced in Northern California. However, this time it was the lack of water from the 1863–64 drought and abundance of gophers that killed his dream. Briggs became disillusioned with his endeavor after two years of farming. He lost a majority of his trees when "a veritable avalanche of gophers descended upon the newly planted trees."[12] It has been reported that Briggs lost his wife and returned to Northern California in 1864. However, the name of Emma as his spouse appears in the 1860, 1870 and 1880 censuses, so this motivation does not appear to be the case.

It's likely he may not have spent much time in Santa Paula in the first place. Building supplies would have been hard to obtain when he first arrived, and he may have returned to Yolo County after the trees were planted. His nephew Jefferson Crane arrived at the same time, and he most likely oversaw their development.

Briggs sold the oil and mineral rights in 1864 to his brother-in-law Edward Wilder Haskell, who was married to his sister Marie Antoinette Briggs. Haskell paid George Briggs $500 on December 24, 1864, and

Haskell received the oil rights as well as any land surplus for the four leagues that Briggs owned.

In the fall of 1866, Elijah B. Higgins purchased the four leagues from Briggs. However, Higgins acted as Briggs's land agent and was to have as his profit all the money over a specified amount.[13] It's likely that at this time Briggs realized his Southern California fruit would not ripen early enough to beat the Northern California market. Higgins had the rancho surveyed in January 1867 by W.H. Norway. From this point, Higgins offered, "The liberal terms upon which he offered it for sale was the principal cause of the first uprising of farmlands in the state, and the general immigration to Southern California. This was the first grant cut up and offered for settlement."[14]

Jefferson Crane was interviewed years later and offered his version: "In the year 1867, George G. Briggs contracted with E.B. Higgins that the last named party might subdivide and colonize the Rancho Santa Paula y Saticoy. I believe this to be the first subdivision of a large land holding in Southern California. Under this contract, the ranch was divided into 150 acre lots."[15]

Briggs moved to Oakland and later to Davisville (Davis) in Yolo County, just north of Sacramento, where he had a four-hundred-acre ranch. He also owned a vineyard of four hundred acres on the American River, another four-hundred-acre property in Woodland and a six-thousand-acre ranch in Fresno where he grew grapes and produced raisins.

By July 1867, the first of the Santa Paula tracts had been sold. John Boyle and Peter Boyle purchased 75 acres each for $480 a parcel. William K. Blanchard bought 150 acres on July 1, 1867, for $960. Also on July 1, Briggs sold Charles O'Hara 150 acres for $1,100. William McCormack purchased 75 acres for $480. On July 24, William Montgomery purchased 80 acres for $1,000. Montgomery soon sold his acreage to Jacob Gries. Gries arrived in the area in 1869 along with James Young Saviers, who purchased land on the Colonia Rancho from Thomas Bard. Gries soon moved to the south side of the river as well.

Briggs and Higgins sold several more tracts in 1867, including 150 acres on August 6 to Elish Larson for $860. On November 26, the deed was recorded for James Tucker for two parcels totaling 182 acres. J.P. Chrisman purchased 368 acres for $3,500 on the same date. By May 1876, his ranch was on the market.

Of the nine people who purchased these first properties, only Elish Larson was still farming ten years later. His is the only deed to also include Briggs and Higgins as "grantors."

One person who arrived in Santa Paula in 1867 but did not purchase land from Briggs was George Richardson. Richardson was from Maine and later lived in Michigan before coming to the gold rush state in 1852. He was able to find 160 acres of government land near the Santa Clara River. With a lumberyard and wharf a few years away, Richardson built an adobe residence he lived in for the next thirty years.

Just prior to the Santa Paula y Saticoy rancho was being surveyed and subdivided, Christian Borchard and his son John Edward "Ed" Borchard were searching for land in the southern portion of the state. Christian Borchard was from Nesselröden, Lower Saxony, Germany. Borchard traveled to the gold fields of Northern California before settling in San Joaquin valley to farm and raise stock. After the floods of 1866 wiped out his livelihood, he traveled south and ended up on the south side of the Santa Clara River. He and his son John Edward Borchard leased land from Jose Lobero. The Borchards planted thirty acres of barley and thirty acres of wheat in March 1867. They soon realized the wheat was susceptible to rust, while the barley flourished. Their date of arrival comes from the roll taken at the inaugural Pioneer Society meeting in 1891. As reported in the *Ventura Signal*, J.E. Borchard's arrival date is listed as March 2, 1867.

With the success of the thirty acres of barley, Christian Borchard pursued the purchase of the La Colonia land. On October 28, 1867, Borchard paid Jose Lobero $3,200 for one thousand acres. Lobero was originally from Italy and used his musical abilities to travel. He landed in Santa Barbara, where original grantee Rafael Gonzalez lived a few blocks away on Laguna Street in the adobe he built in 1825. In 1866, Lobero purchased a portion of Gonzalez's share of the rancho. Lobero would later establish the Lobero Theater, California's earliest opera house. However, at this time Lobero owned a saloon and billiards parlor on Canon Perdido Street in Santa Barbara. Here he may have met up with Gonzalez to conduct their business transactions.

Joining the Borchards at this time in 1867 were Gottfried and Sophie Maulhardt along with Christian's nephew Caspar Borchard. They took up residence in the old Gonzalez adobe, "casa viejo."

Soon after, Gottfried and Caspar began leasing Colonia land from Juan Camarillo. Camarillo purchased several thousand acres from Gonzalez as well.

Meanwhile, Thomas Bard reiterated to Thomas Scott in another letter in April 1867 that he was determined to return home to Pennsylvania. Then he met with Captain W.E. Greenwell of the Coast and Geodetic Survey and the two camped out together for a few days. Greenwell pointed out to Bard the desirable qualities of the area that became Point Hueneme for a wharf site. With the Borchards introducing farming on the Colonia and with the subdividing of Santa Paula and Saticoy, the future of the area was changing. Thomas Bard withdrew his resignation request in May and began his plans to build a wharf near the former Chumash resting ground Wynema to accommodate his next venture of subdividing the large ranchos into smaller ranches.

Bard's first sale went to Michael Kaufman on November 2, 1868, for 160 acres. Kaufman's five daughters were as big an asset as his newly acquired acreage. Each would marry into a prominent farming family that would unite hundreds of cousins for decades to come. Among the families the Kaufman sisters married included John Edward Borchard, who married Mary Kaufman; Fridolyn Hartman married Kathryn Kaufman; Justin Petit married Frances Kaufman; and Louis Pfeiler married Carolyn Kaufman. A fifth daughter, Lizzie, was estranged from the family after an altercation with her mother and Lizzie's abrupt marriage to the Kaufmans' foreman Joseph King.

William De Forest Richards arrived in the Saticoy area in 1868 and purchased six hundred acres.[16] He raised a variety of crops over the years, starting with barley; then flaxseed; canary and bird seed; and later hops, sugar beets and onions. A portion of his ranch became the town of Saticoy.

Sales were slow but steady. Other early farmers included Alexander Gray, who arrived in Santa Paula to take care of the orchard of George Briggs. He is given credit for building the one of the first wooden houses in 1867. In addition to caring for Briggs's orchard, Gray purchased twenty-five acres, where he planted a small orchard of a variety of trees.

In November 1871, Higgins advertised five thousand acres of rich, well-watered land in the Santa Clara Valley for rent or sale. He sold nine hundred acres to George Sewell in 1872.

Higgins's biggest sale, 2,700 acres, occurred in May 1872, when he sold to Nathan Blanchard. The paper reported that Blanchard purchased one-half of Higgins's remaining portion of Rancho Santa Paula y Saticoy for $6,000.[17] Blanchard sold his half to Elisha Lavoyette Bradley. They formed the partnership of Blanchard & Bradley. Bradley remained in Northern California, and Blanchard immediately got to work by ordering the material for the construction of a flour mill. He hired Ed T. Hare to lay out the town site of Santa Paula in November 1873, and the map was recorded on June 16, 1875.[18] Blanchard next partnered with Dana B.

Clark, who planted the first orange orchard of one hundred acres using Havana seedling oranges. The workforce was supplemented "by a number of well-trained and loyal Chinamen."[19]

Higgins retained two hundred acres and planted 3,300 walnut trees and two hundred acres of orange trees.[20] He also built the first gristmill in the area. He later turned to sheep herding.

Bard's biggest sale of Rancho Colonia land was to J.D. Patterson from New York. Patterson purchased nearly six thousand acres for grazing purposes as well as barley production. Among the early ranch hands to work at the Patterson Ranch were Charles J. Daily, his brother Wendell and their father, Charles Wesley Daily. Charles J. Daily was soon promoted to foreman of the ranch. The Daily brothers eventually purchased several acres in Camarillo, where they became innovative farmers and community leaders.

Also working at the Patterson ranch were George and Herbert Eastwood, each earning thirty-five dollars a month. Herbert eventually entered public service as a council member in 1909, and in 1920, he became the mayor of Oxnard, serving a second term in 1942.

Other early farmers who purchased acreage from Bard in 1869 included Jacob Gries and James Saviers ,who bought 682 acres at $15.00 an acre;

Threshing barley on the six-thousand-acre Patterson Ranch on the Oxnard Plain. Barley preceded lima beans as a dry farming crop and paved the way the transition. *Jeff Maulhardt.*

Peter Donlon bought 533 acres at $13.25; William I. Rice paid $13.50 for 1,762 acres; and James Leonard purchased 1,000 acres from Bard, but after the boundaries were reestablished, he received 838 acres. Dominick McGrath received 1,337 acres of the 877 he originally purchased.

Many of the early farmers leased their land before having enough money to purchase. This was the case for Jacob Maulhardt and Gottfried Maulhardt and Johannes Borchard. The Maulhardt brothers traveled from Germany in 1867 to escape the Prussian wars and join Christian Borchard in California. When Borchard was flooded out of his Northern California land in 1866, the group traveled to the unfarmed land of what became the Oxnard Plain. The Maulhardts leased 1,200 acres from Juan Camarillo for $0.50 per acre, and on December 23, 1872, while still part of the soon-to-be-partitioned Santa Barbara County, the three immigrants paid $12,310, or $10 an acre, to Juan Camarillo. Camarillo had purchased several thousand acres from Juan Gonzalez in 1864.

These first farmers grew mostly barley and corn, with many of the larger ranches raising sheep and hogs. However, wild mustard covered the uncultivated land. Christian Borchard took full advantage of the invasive plant. There are several theories on how the black mustard was introduced to Southern California. The most common belief is that Franciscan friars spread the seed to mark the trails that became the El Camino Real, while many of the trails date back to the Chumash, who traveled them for centuries. Another theory on how the plant was propagated was from the importing of sheep and cattle that carried the seed in their fur or stuck to their hide.

The sight of the wild mustard plant rising six feet in the air and covering miles of uncultivated land was an encouraging sign for the first farmers looking to plant a new life. After modifying a Mayberry grain header, Christian Borchard harvested 25 tons of wild mustard plant at $0.02 a pound. In 1870, he produced 5,710 sacks—which weighed 265 tons— garnering a profit of $1,075 and bumping him into the top ten listed in the *Products of Industry in Ventura County.*

In 1870, establishing a needed shipping point was first attempted by W. Barnard. He formed the Wynema Lighter Company with Charles Bailey, Christopher Christenson and Daniel Dempsey. The small, flat-bottomed barge boats anchored at the shore were able to float goods to and fro. Their first shipment arrived in May 1870. Later, this partnership's warehouse would be filled with lima beans.

In competition with Barnard was Thomas Bard. Bard, along with Royce G. Surdam and A.J. Salisbury, formed the Hueneme Wharf and Lighter

Company in February 1871. By August 1871, Bard's 900-foot wharf had been completed, and less than two months later his warehouse was ready for produce to be shipped. The warehouse was located at the front end of a wharf that measured 60 by 200 feet. Within the decade, Bard added two more warehouses with a capacity of ten thousand tons each, and the wharf was extended to 1,500 feet.

In Ventura, Einstein and Bernheim built a warehouse, as did A. Gandolfo.

In the spring of 1878, the *Ventura Free Press* published a series of articles that chronicled the locations of all of the ranches in Ventura County. The *Ventura Signal* answered with a report the following January. These two were combined for a *Quarterly* publication by the Ventura County Museum of History and Art in 2002. From these pages, the following information can be shared to show the condition of agriculture in the first decade of farming in the 1870s.

For Ventura County in 1879, there were 39,000 acres planted to barley; 16,000 acres in corn; 10,000 acres planted to wheat; and 1,700 acres in beans.

Also present among many farms were livestock, including 8,250 hogs in the west county alone. Sheep were also abundant. The Patterson ranch had 2,500; Henry Arnold 1,100; Thomas Rice and Jack Hill raised 2,076 sheep; Christian Borchard 1,000 sheep; Doolittle, Metcalf & Co raised 5,000 sheep on a large portion of the Guadalasca Rancho they leased from William Broome; Henry Arnold on the Conejo 1,100; Johannes Borchard 1,000; the Arnolds 1,100; H.W. Mills 1,200 sheep; and Blanchard and Bradley 2,000 sheep.

The *Ventura Signal* series of articles was much more detailed and showed a growth of activity in the eight months since the rival paper's publication. The livestock count was growing with 24,000 head of hogs; 55,000 sheep; 1,000 Angora goats; 2,000 horses; and 1,400 cattle. Dominick McGrath added 1,200 sheep to his river-bordering land, as did John Scarlett, who added 1,500 head of sheep.

Humble beginning is something else these articles pointed out. Jacob Maulhardt's "model ranch" was described to include 405 acres, 240 acres in barley, 25 acres of corn, fifty tons of pumpkins, fifty head of hogs, two hundred chickens, thirty-eight horses and geese plus 3 acres of fruit trees and a two-year-old vineyard of 1 acre of a choice variety of imported grapevines. He also built a home at a cost of $3,000 that contained a dancing hall of fifteen by twenty-four feet. The writer concluded: "Our purpose in thus going into details is the illustrate what may be done in Ventura County buy a little pluck and well directed energy; a few years ago Mr. Maulhardt came here with a wife and three children and not a cent in his pocket; he rented the land the first year at fifty cents per acre and went to work; next he bought 400 acres, paying $10 an acre."

Martin Laurent also started out renting from Thomas Bard. In 1879, he planted the majority to barley and five acres to corn and six acres to wheat.

Dominick McGrath was ranching seven hundred acres at the time and would add several more ranches over the years to give the family the distinction of the longest continuous farm family in the county. This portion of land was passed down from original land grantee Rafael Gonzalez to his son Ramon, who sold the land to William Rice in 1868. Rice then passed the property on to his son Archibald Rice, who sold to Dominick McGrath on May 1874 for $12,000. By 1879, Dominick had three hundred acres in barley at twenty sacks an acre with the balance in grazing land. He had 1,200 head of sheep, 20 American horses, 300 hogs, 20 head of cattle and a twenty-five-by-forty-foot barn.

John Scarlett from Ireland farmed 700 acres next to the Santa Clara River, of which he cleared 40 acres for farming. He raised 350 acres in barley and 6 acres in corn, 1,500 head of sheep, 12 American horses and 300 hogs, plus "cows enough to supply his table with plenty of milk, cream and butter."

Scarlett also had a well that was originally drilled by William Rice; it was thirty feet deep and sent a seven-inch stream of water over the top of the pipe, which was ten feet above ground. The overflow ran through the adjoining McGrath ranch and formed a deep lake a half mile long and one hundred feet wide, on which a boat was kept for duck hunting.

James Leonard farmed 1,000 acres, and his ranch contained an immense barn of forty by seventy-five feet, a granary and seven buildings in all that the paper described "has more of the resemblance of a village than the home of a quiet farmer." Leonard had 700 acres in cultivation and threshed nine thousand sacks of barley from 450 acres with 80 acres in corn, one hundred head of hogs, thirty head of cattle and forty good horses. Leonard is also credited with building the first wood frame home on the Oxnard Plain in 1868.

Mark McLoughlin farmed 350 acres with 160 acres in barley and produced two thousand sacks, 20 acres of corn, seventy-five hogs, fifteen head of cattle and one hundred fruit trees of different varieties.

Peter Donlon had 300 acres in barley, 20 acres in alfalfa, 15 acres of corn for his three hundred hogs, sixteen horses, a sixteen-by-forty-foot granary, a forty-by-eighty-foot barn and a two-story house with a balcony running around the second story. Peter Donlon married Catherine "Kate"

Cloyne, both from Derry Shanogue, County Longford, Ireland. They traveled to the United States during the potato famine in Ireland in the 1840s and landed in New York. They settled in Dublin, California, in Alameda County. Peter ran a hotel. In 1870, Peter sold his holdings and bought 533 acres from Thomas Bard for $13.25 an acre near the town of Wynema (Hueneme). The property boarded present-day Ventura Road on the west near the Naval Battalion Base to Saviers Road on the east. Within ten years, Peter Donlon was cultivating 300 acres of barley, 15 acres of corn, 20 acres of alfalfa with three hundred hogs and plenty of horses and cows on the ranch. Like most ranches, he also planted 2 acres with a variety of fruit.

Thomas Cloyne farmed 180 acres in barley and rented an additional 120 acres from Hollister for barley and 20 acres of corn for his 100 hogs. He also had 1,400 head of fine stock, most likely sheep. He built a thirty-two-by-sixty-four-foot barn.

The Donlon Brothers threshing outfit on the Thomas Cloyne Ranch on the Colonia, 1896. Cloyne was married to Catherine Donlon and worked for her brother Peter Donlon, eventually purchasing up to one thousand acres in the county. *Museum of Ventura County, photograph 404 OS.*

Anton Maulhardt grew 300 acres in barley, 25 acres to barley hay, 45 acres in corn and 100 tons of pumpkins. Cyrus Snodgrass planted 140 acres to barley, 20 acres to corn and a 400-tree orchard of a variety of fruits and raised 400 hogs.

Thomas Rice farmed 470 acres in barley and another 900 acres with John Hill. He also had 150 in corn, 12 Morgan horses and an additional 100 head of horse and 2,500 head of sheep in partnership with Hill. Thomas A Rice was born in Jackson County, Missouri, in 1849. His parents, William and Louise Rice, came west in 1859, driving 1,000 head of cattle along the way. They settled in Contra Costa County, where the parents remained. However, William purchased several thousand acres of land from the Gonzalez family, of the original grantee, in the late 1860s. By 1870, sons William Ish Rice and his brother Archibald Rice were farming near the river bottom. Thomas Rice relocated to the area in 1883. His father, William Rice Sr., purchased another 338 acres from James Saviers, which was given to Thomas. This property would later become the grounds for the Oxnard Sugar Factory. Thomas Rice owned an additional 900 acres located off current Rice Avenue, between the 101 highway and near Fifth Street. He had a fishpond that was sometimes used by the Pleasant Valley Baptist Church for their baptism ceremonies.

James Young Saviers raised nine hundred acres of barley and seven hundred acres of wheat on the Simi Rancho. He also put in two hundred acres of corn and had three acres of orchard and five hundred grapevines plus strawberries, and his ranch sported a blacksmith shop. Saviers arrived in Santa Barbara County in October 1869. James's wife, Mattie, was active in helping make their place a model ranch. They soon realized they needed relief from the strong winds that could easily wipe out a summer's crop. About the same time as Ellwood Cooper was importing eucalyptus in the Santa Barbara/Goleta area. Mattie helped establish a nursery at the ranch and began importing red and blue gum trees that served as the first set of windbreaks in the county. Saviers also built a massive barn, forty-eight by seventy feet, big enough to store ninety tons of hay and stable thirty-eight horses.

Louis Pfeiler grew 240 acres in barley and 50 acres in corn. He had a neatly painted cottage surrounded by blue gums, pepper and cypress trees. He also grew 60 acres of fine grapevines. His home was later relocated to downtown Oxnard as part of Heritage Square.

Michael Kaufman cultivated 320 acres, with 300 acres in barley and 20 acres in corn. Caspar Borchard grew 140 acres in barley and raised 160 hogs and rented an additional 85 acres in to grow corn.

Johannes (John) Borchard, cousin to John Edward Borchard and brother to Caspar Borchard, came over in 1871 from Werxhausen, Germany. He traveled with his wife and two sons only to lose his six-year-old after a rough Atlantic Ocean crossing and then burying his nine-month-old upon their arrival in the area. Yet he went on to donate the land for the original St. John's Hospital in Oxnard along with a donation of $20,000 to help build the hospital in 1914. Back in 1879, John farmed four hundred acres that produced 3,669 sacks of barley and raised 1,300 sheep.

His neighbor to the north was Gottfried Maulhardt, who sold two hundred acres of his four-hundred-acre ranch to Caspar Borchard yet was able to plant the majority in barley at twenty sacks an acre. His cottage is the only remaining house from this period and was described thus: "His neat little cottage house is hid away among acacias and other ornamental; trees and flowers. An abundance of water is raised by an Althouse windmill. It carried up into a 4000 gallon tank, 30 feet high." Also included in the description is another connection to the history of the area. Many of the early farmers were of Catholic faith and attended the Mission church in Ventura. Due to the long ride and the hazards associated with crossing the bridge-less Santa Clara River to get there, the growing farming community to the south of the river banded together to build a Catholic church. Gottfried, along with his brothers Jacob and Anton and Christian Borchard and Dominick McGrath, formed the building committee to get the project accomplished. To accommodate the church services, Gottfried Maulhardt erected a brick building in his property to serve as a winery. An article in the *Ventura Signal* of January 11, 1879, confirms Gottfried's association with the story when it published the following description in the same article: "A small vineyard of 250 grapevines of the choicest varieties."

Though the vineyards did not survive into the twenty-first century, the winery and the house have. They have become part of the Oxnard Historic Farm Park, given the address 1251 Gottfried Place, Oxnard. To connect the winery with the past, the Foundation for the Farm Park secured zinfandel cuttings from the vineyards on Santa Cruz Island that date back to the 1880s.

The largest of the ranches was the Patterson Ranch, nearly 6,000 acres owned by J.D. Patterson from New York. A portion of the ranch was farmed in 1878 by John H. Thompson, and the remainder was run by Mr. Cook and a few years later by Charles J. Daily. At this time, close to 1,000 acres were considered wasteland due to the marshy conditions. Cook was able to plant 1,000 acres in barley and 160 acres in corn and stocked 2,500 sheep, 1,500 hogs and "a considerable number of horses."

Across the Santa Clara River from Ventura to Santa Paula were smaller yet numerous farms as reported in 1878.[21] Barley and corn were the top two crops, with 7,287 acres and 8,490 acres, respectively. There were 1,251 acres planted in beans, but this would have included limas, green beans and castor beans. There were also 582 acres in orchards and smaller plantings of canary seed, flax, wheat and potatoes. The other big farming operation was raising hogs, and at this time, there were approximately eighteen thousand head.

The two larger areas in the lower Ventura side were the Olivas and Dixie W. Thompson ranches, both consisting of 2,400 acres. Olivas rented out the majority of his acreage, and Thomson raised 400 acres of barley, 500 acres of corn and one thousand hogs.

Other large-scale farming was done by Gilpin Chrisman and James Willoughby. Chrisman farmed 640 acres in east Ventura and along with Willoughby farmed 300 acres of corns and another 330 acres of barley and 200 acres of pumpkins and beans and 250 hogs on land rented from the Olivas family.

James A. Day, Sherlock Bristol and Aratus Everett were also successful farmers in the Ventura/Montalvo area. Day farmed 230 acres and planted 50 acres in fruit, 80 acres of barley and 100 acres of corn to feed his 350 head of hogs.

Lima bean threshing on the six-thousand-acre Patterson Ranch. Charles Daily served as foreman of the ranch before purchasing land in Camarillo, where he continued farming. *Eric Daily.*

Sherlock Bristol, a farmer and pastor for the Congregational Church, arrived in the area in 1868 and purchased 120 acres. In addition to growing barley and corn, he planted apples, apricots, pears, almonds, oranges and peaches.

Everett also came in 1868 and partnered with Jonathon Mayhew from Santa Barbara. He farmed three hundred acres of Mayhew's property in Montalvo and two hundred acres of the Olivas tract. He grew barley and corn and raised one thousand Poland China hogs.

Next to Day's ranch was the Kelsey Brothers property. Theodore and Joseph Kelsey farmed three hundred acres, of which two hundred were dedicated to growing beans.

Near Saticoy, Eugene Duval farmed 25 acres with fruit trees and barley, and his son Charles farmed an additional 60 acres. Benjamin and Frank Dudley owned 40 acres and at this time grew exclusively corn. George Kimball farmed 75 acres, and Jefferson Crane farmed 200 acres of barley, corn and beans. William de Forrest Richards owned 375 acres in Saticoy and devoted a large portion to growing flax. The town of Saticoy also evolved from a portion of his property. Near Richards's property was 600 acres owned by Reverend Samuel T. Wells, a Presbyterian pastor. He leased the land to Silvanus White, who lived on the farm, with 350 acres pastured in hogs, 120 acres in corn, 40 acres in barley and a small quantity of apples and other fruit trees.

George Washington Faulkner came to the county in 1876 and farmed near El Rio on the Del Norte before purchasing his 150-acre ranch off West Telegraph and Briggs Road. Faulkner was planted one of the first walnut orchards and was one of the first to plant lima beans.

Marquis de Lafayette Todd farmed 90 acres next to Telegraph Road, where he raised corn, barley, pumpkins and a 10-acre orchard. John Franklin Cummings's farm was opposite of Todd's place and consisted of 150 acres with orange and lemon trees as well as barley corn and alfalfa. East of Todd was Allen Hedrick, who grew 40 acres of barley, pumpkins, corn and potatoes plus an orchard of one hundred trees.

Abner Haines grew lemons, oranges, walnuts, various fruit trees and alfalfa, and he also raised horses and hogs.

Bean harvesting on the Faulkner Farm in Santa Paula. George Washing Faulkner arrived in the county in 1876. He was one of the first to grow apricots and walnuts. *Alison Ayers O'Neill and Craig Held.*

C.C Newell farmed nine hundred acres near the foothills, where he planted three hundred orange and lemon trees and a nursery of twenty thousand blue gum trees. He also raised corn and hogs.

Elijah B. Higgins partnered with George Briggs to sell portions of the rancho and retained two hundred acres that he planted to citrus; he also grew barley and corn and raised hogs—the norm of the day.

Nathan Blanchard arrived in 1872 and purchased 2,700 acres and is credited with planting the first orange orchard of eight thousand trees on 100 acres. He also built a flour mill. He raised 1,500 hogs and 2,500 sheep.

While barley remained a staple crop for the early farmers, they were always on the lookout for a crop that would bring in more income. The introduction of lima beans to Ventura County started a long and successful tenure in Ventura County.

3

LIMAS COME TO VENTURA COUNTY

The first printed reference to anyone growing lima beans in Ventura County was in 1871, when the *Santa Barbara Weekly Press* reported in the May 27 edition that Captain Jonathon Mayhew, who lived at the Light House in Santa Barbara, had planted one hundred acres of beans on his property in the Santa Clara Valley. This property was located in the Montalvo area. His foreman was Aratus Mayhew. The story is that he sold the seeds for four cents a pound. Mayhew and Everett turned their efforts toward raising hogs, Poland China swine. They would eventually fence in three hundred acres and raise 1,200 hogs. Everett would branch out in later years and purchase land in Moorpark, where he successfully grew apricots.

The *Ventura Signal* was advertising the benefits of the lima bean as early as February 3, 1872. The *Signal* editor claimed they were the "best beans ever grown and they cook quickly and are rich are well flavored and command double the price in the new our market of any other bean."

Jefferson Crane planted 160 acres of limas in 1874. Crane came to Southern California from Ohio in 1861, a month after marrying Jeanette Briggs. She was the daughter of George C. Briggs, who purchased nearly seventeen thousand acres of the Santa Paula/Saticoy Rancho from Thomas More. Crane contacted a friend in New York to sell his beans, but he had little luck in selling the beans. Soon after, Crane's father, George Washington Crane, who lived in Ohio, followed up and personally peddled the beans to multiple East Coast cities. The popularity of the beans began to take hold, and a market was created.[22]

James Allen Day of East Ventura had an eighty-acre farm that was planted in citrus and other trees, but by 1875, he was selling lima and butler beans from his ranch.[23] Theodore and Joseph Kelsey bought the three hundred acres of the Jack Hill Ranch in Montalvo in 1876. As an experiment, the Kelsey brothers planted twenty acres of lima beans. The crop was so successful that they planted the entire three hundred acres to lima bean plus an additional one hundred acres, the largest acreage of lima beans ever planted in the county at this time. However, the brothers only received between two and three cents per pound. Also, harvesting at this time consisted of hand hooks to cut the beans and the use of horses to break open the pods. This method proved too time-consuming and not profitable. They continued farming beans a few more years before selling the land and turning to growing walnuts.

Jefferson Crane came to the Santa Paula y Saticoy rancho with his uncle George Briggs, who purchased the land in 1862. Crane helped develop the lima bean industry. *Santa Paula Historical Society.*

By 1878, beans were beginning to take hold on the Colonia, with one thousand acres planted to beans. However, these beans consisted of small white beans, Bayo beans and lima beans. Henry Flint planted one of the larger plots at forty acres. Jefferson Crane grew two hundred acres of lima beans in Saticoy.

Beans were also beginning to take hold from Ventura to Santa Paula. While barley and corn dominated the plantings with a combined 16,000 acres, bean acreage was up to 1,251 acres.

On January 18, 1879, it was reported that Jonathon Mayhew raised barley, peas, corn and lima beans on his 76-acre ranch near the Olivas ranch in the Mound District. Marion Cannon grew beans on 20 acres of his 165-acre ranch in Saticoy. His neighbor Jacob Holland raised 300 sacks of beans. Charles Finney planed 40 acres in beans and produced 180 acres from 15 acres. George Genella produced 1,100 sacks of beans. M. Swall grew 15 acres of beans. George Rostler grew 36 acres in beans on land he rented from Eugene Duval that yielded 39,000 pounds. Charles Kimball planted 14 acres to beans that produced 1,200 pounds an acre. Judge Wason grew 15 acres that produced 250 sacks. T.J. Criss grew lima beans that sold for fifty cents per hundred pounds. R.M. Haydock grew a large quantity of beans. Juan and Ignacio Rodriguez raised beans on their 400 acres plus hay and vegetables, and Jose Moraga grew 40 acres to beans.

Other than a few acres here and there, lima beans were still several years away from taking over Ventura County. In December 1880, A.D. Barnard began advertise the sale of lima bean seed. Among his claims was that it was an early variety, first time in the market and a prolific bearer in adobe or sandy soil. The ad must have worked, because Judge Hines of Ventura County was quoted in the *Bakersfield California* in December 1881 that the principal crops of the area were grain and lima beans and the average yield of the two crops for farmers averaged one hundred dollars an acre. They were "so rich, prosperous and independent that they look with pity upon men holding official positions and the mercantile class."

In April 1882, Alex Gandolfo, who owed a mercantile store near the mission San Buenaventura, advertised "choice select seed Lima Beans."

George Faulkner from Santa Paula planted his lima beans on May 4, 1882, and threshed the beans on September 27, 1882.[24] By October 21, he had tramped the dried beans and cleaned them before taking them to Mr. Wolivers (Wooliver or Woolever). Like many of the early farmers, he also grew wheat, barley, corn, apples, potatoes and other crops, looking for the one that would pay the bills.

W.L. Dodge completed a three-month effort to build a bean thresher that he demonstrated to the public in November 1883.

The spring of 1884 was a wet one, and because there was so much moisture in the soil, the beans stayed green and ripened late for harvest.

In 1885, Jefferson Crane improved his bean thresher so as not to break the beans in the process. A pamphlet published by Bowers and Sons stated that the population of Ventura was nearing two thousand and lima beans could produce as many as two thousand pounds an acre. Thomas Gabbert, who farmed the R.C. Sudden place, produced a large crop of lima beans.

James Clay rented twenty acres to farm lima beans in 1886 near Santa Paula and made $1,359.50. Another farmer from Santa Paula named Hudeberg (Hudiburg) planted ninety acres and cleared $2,000.

Achille Levy, a produce broker in Hueneme, was a member of the San Francisco Produce Exchange and had a respectable knowledge of the market value of produce. Levy received word from his connections in the Midwest that a new strain of barley was being developed and that the market value of the price of barley would decrease. Levy was known to spend up to $200 on Western Union communications to stay on top of the market.[25] News of the certain drop in barley prices alerted Levy to keep his eye on a replacement crop. Levy soon placed an ad in the local paper advertising the sale of the beans for planting.

By 1887, close to six thousand acres were planted in Bayo, castor, small white and lima beans resulting in 4,500 tons or 140,000 bags.[26] C.H. McKevett planted eighty acres in limas on his three-hundred-acre ranch near Santa Paula. The Patterson ranch, under the supervision of Charles J. Daily, planted enough beans to bring in $58,000, which equates to over $1 million in today's dollars. Jefferson Crane and the Dixie Thompson's thresher began harvesting by late September.

The sons of Henry Lewis from Carpenteria were instrumental in introducing commercial planting of lima beans to Ventura County. William Leachman, Dozier and Joseph Lewis were young boys when their father first planted lima beans in 1868. They helped their father plant, harvest and select the best-producing lima bean plants.

Oldest son William Leachman Lewis was the first to venture out in 1885. He borrowed money to buy teams of horses and farming implements. He rented a parcel near Santa Paula and after four years was able to pay off his debt and purchased a good six-horse team from the Patterson Ranch at the cost of $1,000. He then introduced lima beans to the Colonia Rancho on the south side of the Santa Clara River by leasing part of the Scarlett ranch, becoming one of the first commercial growers of lima beans in the county.[27]

Joseph Lewis was the first to plant lima beans in the Camarillo district in 1889. He rented two hundred acres from Martina Camarillo, mother of Juan and Adolfo Camarillo. John Benn also came from Carpinteria to grow beans in Camarillo.

At the same time, the Dixie Thompson Ranch on the north side of the Santa Clara River also planted a large section to lima beans. Under the recommendations and guidance of the superintendent of the ranch, James Milligan, the Thompson ranch planted 400 acres. However, because of some unexpected wet weather, he was able to harvest only about 250 acres.

The Dixie Thompson ranch was originally part of Rancho San Miguel originally owned by the Raymundo Olivas. Thompson purchased half of the western portion of the rancho, 2,400 acres, in 1864. The massive ranch was not always perceived in a positive light by the local press. A headline in *Ventura Weekly Post and Democrat* on September 9, 1892, declared "A PUBLIC ENEMY—Dixie Thompsons Bean Ranch a Deadly Detriment to Ventura's Progress." The article rants about the greed of Thompson and frustration about the city's inability to grow or collect more tax dollars. Despite the paper rant, Thompson's ranch continued to grow into the largest bean farm in the world.

Thompson's relationship with the city slowly improved, as he donated a portion of his land for streets and improvements. He was also known for his famous horse, Tecumseh, which he rode in many events over the years. Thompson was also known for his elegant silver-mounted saddle and bridle.

J.B. Alvord from the New Jerusalem area (north Oxnard) also planted beans in 1889, planting 180 acres that averaged one ton an acre and some that produced three tons per acre. John Edward Borchard, who farmed near Alvord, planted 67 acres to limas and produced 1,736 sacks at 1,950 pounds per acre.

In the Saticoy and Ventura area, several farmers planted beans. J.C. Philips from Saticoy planted 260 acres. T. Bither farmed 100 acres. W.F. and J.R. Willoughby of Ventura planted 150 acres. T.W. Price planted 40 acres in beans. John Darling, referred to as a jolly Scotchman, planted 150 acres. George Butler was called an enterprising Englishman. James Evans planted 108 acres; S.J. and J.H. Alexander planted 80 acres.[28] T.S. Kelsey also planted beans, barley and potatoes. G.G. Crane, five years removed from Ohio, planted 50 acres to walnuts with rows of lima beans between the trees.

A John Calvin Brewster photograph of threshing beans in Saticoy, circa 1900. *Museum of Ventura County, photograph 17234.*

47

Peter Rice and Robert Bell from the Callegues Rancho also grew a quantity of lima beans in 1889. The prediction for the year was eight hundred tons. The new crop was firmly planted in the county.

The word was spreading on the payoff on planting lima beans. The *Hueneme Herald* made a proclamation in November 1889 that proved true: "There is every indication that a large area of lands heretofore sown to barley will be planted in beans this coming season."

After a year on the Scarlett ranch, William Leachman Lewis moved one ranch east and rented from James Leonard. Lewis paid Leonard one-third of his crop as rent. By the end of the season, he had more than enough for rent and more. The Lewis brothers trampled 1,200 sacks of beans and then hired the Hund, Ayers and Johnston thresher No. 2 to thresh out 2,018 sacks of lima beans. Walter Steele hauled the beans to Montalvo.

The first train load of lima beans to be shipped back east was by Achille Levy of Hueneme via the Southern Pacific and Union Pacific Railroad. Each car carried a banner that read "California beans, shipped by A. Levy, Hueneme, Ventura Cal. wholesale dealer in California products." The original ten cars contained 110 tons of beans, and they passed through Nebraska, Kansas City, Chicago, Philadelphia and New York.

In November 1890, Achille Levy sent twenty-two freight cars from San Pedro to eastern cities. Hanging from the cars were large signs that read: "Bannered Beans from Hueneme, Shipped by A Levy." Thus, Achille Levy earned the title of "Bean King." The beans were shipped by boat to San

Steam tractor pulling lima bean wagons and thresher, circa 1900. *Museum of Ventura County, photograph 15602.*

Pedro and then loaded on train cars destined for New York and Boston. Eventually, nearly one thousand carloads were shipped to the East.

Among Levy's shipment was a crop worth $12,000 paid to Sam Fong Yi, a Chinese contractor from Ventura.[29] Frank Lambardo raised 500 sacks that averaged 72 pounds a sack on eight acres while farming on the Olivas tract. Other growers included H.F. Clark, Montalvo; Sam Guthrie of Springville, who counted over 123 pods from one vine; and Dan Kelly from Hueneme, who vaunted 64 pods containing 185 beans from one of his vines. J.B. Brooks from Pleasant Valley reported he had a vine that was 16 feet long and carried 74 pods with over 200 beans. Robert Sebastian of Springville also grew beans.

The *Ventura Free Press* claimed, "There are no finer fields of limas anywhere in Southern California than on this side of the Santa Clara River." The ranches observed were McGlinchey, Alvord, Maulhardt, Saviers, Gordon and Furrer brothers.

For 1890, Ventura County planted eighteen thousand acres in lima beans that produced 100 million pounds. John Mahan, a prominent rancher of the Springville area, predicted the acreage planted to lima beans would double. The average yield was from 1,000 to 1,500 pounds an acre. Barley was still a large crop, and the planting of walnuts were also on the rise.[30]

The new crop also opened up other areas for farming where farming had not yet been introduced. The majority of the Del Norte Rancho was used for cattle and later sheep crazing, but the abundance of cactus discouraged agriculture. Because of the minimal requirements to plant and grow the beans, the rancho took on a new life. It was announced that for the 1891 year, the entire mesa owned by A. Schiappa Peitra was to be rented out.

With the success of the lima beans, farmers were seeing not only the fruits of their labor but the dollars as well. Several of the established farmers were now in a position to upgrade their residences. John Edward Borchard was able to invest $7,000 for his new two-story "handsome and commodious" residence. To accommodate this wife's sub-five-foot stature, the kitchen counters and cabinets were designed for her convenience.

Others who planned to build new homes on their ranches included J. B. Alvord, Mark McLaughlin, James Fulkerson, the Donlon brothers, G.E. Kaltmeyer, John Cawelti, Michael Flynn and Adolfo Camarillo.

Under the heading "Colonia Items" in the *Ventura Free Press* on May 19, 1891, it was reported that Dozier Lewis planted 240 acres of limas and his brother Wm. Lewis finished putting in 314 acres on the Leonard Ranch.

The Richardson Bros. had about 200 acres of lima beans. Henry and Lee Richardson relocated from Carpinteria. John grew beans on the Scarlett Ranch. James O'Conner planted 125 acres, Joseph Reiman, 80 acres. Hiram K. Snow planted 75 acres in lima beans. Zack Graham had 60 acres in limas; Ed Borchard 50 acres; J.B. Alvord 130 acres; Mark McLoughlin 53 acres; Archie Connelly 60 acres; Will Haydock 60 acres; William R. Snively 40 acres; C.H. Butterfield 30 acres; and J. Grainger 10 acres.

San Pedro District: Thomas Bell planted 100 acres in limas that yielded 2,400 pounds per acre. Thomas Rice planted 80 acres of beans, and Albert Foulks also planted a similar acreage. Mr. Schurtz planted 35 acres.

Hueneme: Thomas Cloyne, 60 acres.

Ocean View Notes: Jacob Maulhardt farmed 300 acres in Ocean View District planted to lima beans; J.M. Dunn, 200 acres; James Fisher, 120 acres; J.C. Cline, 100 acres; G.E. Kaltmeyer, 100 acres; A.C. Vickers, 60 acres; Greville Pidduck, 60 acres; M.H. Arnold, 60 acres; D.O. Hillman, 60 acres; Leroy Arnold, 55 acres; G.A. Hails, 55 acres; Goodyear and Philbrook, 50 acres; Louis Pfeiler, 50 acres; H.I. Hillman, 40 acres; Henry Arnold, 20 acres; J.M. Revolon, 20 acres; August Callens, 20 acres; Thomas Arundel, 28 acres; Ed Gonzales, 15 acres; George Johnson, 15 acres.

Springville: W.A. Lillie, 25 acres in limas; J.B. Palin, 400 acres; Frank Furrer, 120 acres; Oscar Stewart, 70 acres; E.G. Martin, 60 acres; Caspar Wucherpfennig, 10 acres; George Griffiths and sons, 300 acres. Adolfo Camarillo owned 10,000 acres, with 3,000 under cultivation by twelve tenants. On his home tract, Adolfo grew 150 acres of lima beans.

Solari Ranch off Central Avenue, part of the Del Norte Rancho, circa 1915. John Mitchell is standing. Tom Steele was thresher operator. *Museum of Ventura County, photograph 10870 OS.*

Las Posas: A.M. Graham turned out 1,400 pounds of lima beans per acre. Simon Cohn planted on cactus land on his plot on the Del Norte rancho, which the paper claimed never raised anything hitherto.

Montalvo Items: Harry Valentine planted 115 acres for George Cook; J.M Silva, 40 acres; Scott Gibson, 40 acres; R.H. Valentine, 53 ½ acres; Joseph F. Lewis, 290 acres; Shattuck and Stoddard, 200 acres; C.S. Clayton, 30 acres.

Santa Paula: John F. Cummings planted 160 acres of beans, making 3,000 sacks averaging 70 pounds a sack for a total of 210,000 pounds of beans.

In Wheeler Canyon, the Darling Brothers planted twenty to twenty-five acres in lima beans.

The largest grower of lima beans at this time, by far, was D.W. Thompson. By 1891, his ranch was growing 1,200 acres of lima beans. For that year, he was able to send 29,659 sacks of beans weighing a total of 2,011,270 pounds to the Southern Mill & Warehouse Company. This added up to one hundred train cars at 10 tons each. It took eight trains to deliver the beans.

In 1892, Dozier Lewis threshed out two thousand pounds of limas per acre on the Leonard Ranch, which he rented from 1890–93. Hugh Henry from Montalvo took over the lease for the next year, and Lewis moved over to the Scarlett Ranch, which was previously rented to Leo Richardson.

Along with lima beans, the Lady Washington bean was planted at this time. The Washingtons ripened earlier than the limas and were less susceptible to heat. Among the farmers also trying out the Lady Washingtons were B.M. Bynum, August Callens, James Clay, Harry Hooker, John Hegan, F. Lombardo, Jacob Maulhardt, Mark McLoughlin and Lewis Pierano. With time, the limas proved to bring in a higher price.

There were 250 representatives from Ventura County who attended the Chicago World's Fair in May 1893. The majority, nearly 150, came from Ventura and Santa Paula, including E.P. Foster and his wife, Orpha; John McGonigle, the editor of the *Ventura Democrat*; Cephas Bard and wife; Nathan W. Blanchard Sr. and Jr.; G.W. Faulkner; G.N. Ruggles; George Todd; W.D.F. Richards and his wife; Mr. and Mrs. Joseph Kelsey; Marion Cannon; W.L. Hardison; Allen Hedrick; and Albert Ayers. From Hueneme included Achille Levy, Thomas Bard and daughter Berl Bard, Leon Lehman, James Donlon, John McCoy and Dr. Sessions. From New Jerusalem, Oxnard/El Rio area came Zach Graham, William Rice, Gottfried, Sophie and Annie Maulhardt, Adolph Maulhardt, J.B Alvord and his wife.

Cutting limas on the William E. Goodyear Ranch, Somis, circa 1900. Goodyear arrived in the county in 1885 and farmed in Ocean View before purchasing a 180-acre tract in Somis. He married Ida Philbrook, sister of his original partner. *Museum of Ventura County, photograph 8410.*

Workers at the Saticoy Lima Bean Packing House. *Left to right*: Pantaleon "Pompi" Garcia, Adan "Chicano" Macias (*obscured by hat*), Angel Reyes, unidentified, Pedro "Pete" Reyes, unidentified. Beans grown by W.W. Cummings, Santa Paula. *Museum of Ventura County, photograph 31794.*

Many firsts were introduced at the World's Fair, including Quaker Oats, Aunt Jemima Pancake Mix, Cracker Jack, the hamburger, the Chicago hotdog, brownies, ice cream cones, Juicy Fruit gum, Pabst Blue Ribbon beer, the zipper and the Ferris wheel. The representatives from Oxnard were there to promote the lima bean and other produce, including oranges. For the county's exhibit, they created the Ventura County Lima Bean Pagoda, with the word *Ventura* spelled out in colored lima beans in twenty-two different places along with several artistic designs created with the beans. On the roof of the pagoda were sixteen varieties of beans growing in pots of soil from Ventura County. Over two thousand pounds of beans were used with eighty-three varieties. Other products included Washington navel oranges, sundried apricots, nuts and honey. The pagoda was invented by Judge Nehemiah Blackstock, architect George C. Powers and F.A. Foster. Captain W.H. Thompson of Saticoy showed visitors the exhibit. The pagoda was octagonal in shape and measured twenty-three and one-half feet high and twelve feet in diameter. It contained 615 glazed compartments filled with beans.

Above: At the 1893 World's Fair in Chicago, Ventura County built a pagoda display that measured twenty-three and a half feet tall and twelve feet wide and featured two thousand pounds of lima beans with the word *Ventura* spelled out in lima beans. Over 250 residents from the county attended the fair. *Jeff Maulhardt.*

Opposite, top: Threshing in Santa Paula, pre-1900. *Front row, left to right*: Frank Moore, George Washington Faulkner, F.P. McDivitt, Paul McDivitt, Louie (boy), Gladys Henderson, Ted Henderson, William Webber, Sam Henderson, Frank Robbins. *Back row*: C.J. McDivitt, Mr. Thompson, Nettie Bay, Edith McDivitt, Bernice McDivitt (*baby*). *Santa Paula Historical Society.*

Opposite, bottom: Matt Borchard, youngest son of Ed Borchard, cultivating beans off Gonzales Road, Oxnard, circa 1910. *Jeff Maulhardt.*

The year 1894 was a dry one. On the Colonia, Dozier Lewis raised 1,600 pounds an acre. Jacob Maulhardt held his beans over from the previous year, 37,000 sacks, which brought in $10,000. Another one of the few good harvests was also on the Colonia in the San Pedro District. P.S. Carr grew 250 acres and harvested 3,970 sacks averaging 80 pounds a sack at $0.04 per pound worth $12,000. James Milligan, A. Dobbin and Fred Thurston also raised beans in the area.

In the Mound District, William Ready grew beans. In Saticoy, the Crane brothers, T.A. Kelsey and H.W. Gibson all planted beans, some

crops producing better than others. The *Ventura Free Press* reported: "The Chinaman who rents land adjoining C.N. Kimball's place is hauling in and treading out his crop of beans. His crop seems to be an excellent one for this year."

However, over in Montalvo, the same was not the case for Ernest Hill. He decided to abandon the crop, reasoning it was too expensive the hire help to harvest. The Chapman brothers took on the task of pulling the beans. Johnson and Dr. Dempsey planted beans as well.

William Lewis continued farming the McGrath property he had begun leasing two years before. He paid $10 a year per acre for three hundred acres. His crop earned $14,000, allowing Lewis to purchase a lot at the corner of Santa Clara and Kalorama Streets, where he built his retirement home. In 1898, he ran for sheriff on the Republican ticket and lost by two votes to incumbent Paul Charlebois. He next ran successfully for Board of City Trustees, on which he served for eight years, five years as president of the board, making him an early mayor of Ventura.

By 1895, more farmers had dedicated their land to lima beans. The son of J.E. Borchard, Willie, got in on the action by planting the Mammoth bush lima beans for J.B. Alvord. He used a Boss planter and did the work solo.

Workers on the Lloyd Butler Ranch, Del Norte Rancho. *Craig Held.*

The number of varieties of seeds was estimated at 125. The warehouses in the county reported 750 tons at $60 a ton. Dixie Thompson in Montalvo produced 24,000 sacks of beans. The Schiappa Pietra estate on the Del Norte Rancho produced over 100,000 sacks.

The county produced a mere 4,661 sacks in 1873. By 1895, the harvested crop was valued at $1,100,000. It took 2,600 train cars of 10 tons each to transport the beans across the country.[31] With these numbers, the *Ventura Free Press* proclaimed that Ventura County became the "bean producing centre of the world."

More and more was being learned and shared among the farmers about how to use the straw from the bean harvest. J.G. Ricker hauled baled lima bean straw with two four-horse teams from the fields threshed by Dozier Lewis on the Colonia. The straw was then combined with crushed barley to make a good feed for all stock, except for the driving teams. Some farmers used the chaff for fuel for a steam engine if it was a hay burner.

Talk of forming a Lima Bean Association began as early as June 1895 at a meeting with the Walnut Growers Association, which had formed just two years prior. Many of the walnut growers were successfully planting lima beans between the rows of trees, and there was an overlap of interested farmers between to two. G.G. Crane was the chairman and Jefferson Crane the secretary of the Walnut Association. After the Walnut Growers meeting was adjourned, there remained seventy persons of interest to discuss forming the Lima Bean Committee. A committee of eight was appointed to formulate a plan for the organization: Thomas Rice, A. Gillon, George Power, G.C. Crane, David T. Perkins, Nathan Blanchard, James M. Sharp and Jack Hill.

By October 1896, Albert F. Maulhardt, Jacob Maulhardt, M. Cannon, Dozier Lewis, H.F. Clark, P.S. Carr, T.G. Gabbert and J.E. Borchard all joined together to form the Lima Bean Association. The next month, on November 18, the board met in Montalvo and cast votes for the different terms of office. For three-year terms: F.A Hollister of Goleta; J. Bailard, Carpinteria; M.D.L. Todd, Santa Paula. For two-year terms: Mark McLaughlin, Colonia; Jack G. Hill, Hueneme; T.G. Gabbert, El Rio. For a one-year term, George Cooks, Montalvo; Thomas Rice, El Rio; Jacob Maulhardt, El Rio. Thomas Rice was appointed treasurer and Albert F. Maulhardt as secretary.

With an overproduction of the crop, prices for the lima bean were falling fast. The price of lima beans dropped from $0.05 per pound in 1890 to $0.025 cents in 1895.[32] The estimated losses for 1895 were over $1 million.

Threshing lima beans in Ventura County pre-1900. *Pleasant Valley Historical Society.*

The 1896 year was also included an August heat wave that decimated the crops. The *Ventura Free Press* reported on August 21, 1896, that lima beans were drying fast. "Many are already cutting, which is at least a month earlier than usual. They estimate this year's yield at not more than half the crop."

One of the few ranchers who produced a successful crop was Charles Beckwith of Santa Paula. From twenty-two acres, he gathered and threshed 861 sacks averaging 79¾ pounds each or 3,121 pounds per acre. Beckwith planted some of the beans between his apricot trees, and for a three-acre plot, he harvested an even more impressive sacking of 210 sacks at 5,287 pounds to the acre.[33]

To help with prices in the future, a new crop was soon introduced to the county: sugar beets. Albert F. Maulhardt, the aforementioned secretary of the Lima Bean Association, would soon be supervising the planting, cultivating and harvesting of a series of beet plantings over the next two years. The *Venture Free Press* reported:

Nearly two thousand acres will be planted this year to sugar beets, the crop to be shipped to Chino, and if a big sugar factory is established in the county, fully twelve thousand acres will be devoted to their cultivation. This means that the amount of land upon which beans or barley has been therefore grown, will be lessened about that much. This will give better prices for our staple products, and the results obtained the past season from growing sugar beets, insure a good return from land devoted to that industry.

Albert's efforts in helping establish a lima bean industry in the county was pointed out by the *Hueneme Herald*, and the story was picked up by the *Ventura Weekly Post and Democrat*:

> *There is one gentleman, too, who was a prime mover and originator of the movement, and a young gentleman whose energy was in a great measure the cause of its present success and that is our fellow townsman, A.F. Maulhardt. We know what Albert did for the association as well anyone and we would like to see him accorded some of the credit for establishing this new gigantic enterprise.*[34]

Albert was able to help the lima bean farmer by introducing a complementary crop, but he also convinced the Oxnard investors to build a $2 million sugar refinery that spawned the establishment of the town of Oxnard.

Another advantage of two machines connected was the two sacking stations. Carl Borchard's crew is farming off Wolf Road, near Pleasant Valley Road. *Mary Borchard Donlon.*

Ed Borchard and Justin Petit joined forces to purchase a bean thresher as early as 1895. The two families were connected through their wives, Mary and Frances Kaufmann. *Craig Held.*

The majority of the bean growers came on board to support the Lima Bean Association. Thomas Rice turned over his 5,500 sacks of limas. The biggest growers also joined the association, including Dixie Thompson at 33,000 sacks; Schiappa Pietra, 15,000 sacks; and J.D. Patterson, 12,000 sacks.

Ventura County planted eighty kinds of lima beans. Popular lima bean varieties at this time included the Lewis Common, King of the Garden, Large Champion and the Burpee, which are the creeping variety. The Dreer, Rice, Jersey, Mammoth, Henderson and Sieve are the bush variety. The string or snap type includes the Small White and the Lady Washington, the latter being the most cultivated.

Among the threshing outfits at work in October 1896 were Petit and Borchard, J.D. Patterson Ranch, Joseph Lewis, Louis Maulhardt, Donlon Bros. and Richardson and Carr and Charles Spence from Saticoy. Charles Beckwith of Santa Paula produced a record yield. From twenty-two acres, he threshed 861 sacks averaging nearly 80 pounds each, which came out to 3,121 pounds per acre. The majority of the beans were grown between his young apricot trees.

Lima beans were doing so well in Ventura County at this time that farmers in Orange County were taking note. The largest landowner, James Irvine of the Irvine Company, owned over 100,000 acres that he used to grow grains and citrus. He invited two of Ventura County's more influential lima bean leaders, William Lewis and Frank Barnard, to inspect his land for its ability to grow lima beans. Within a few years, Orange County would rival Ventura County for lima bean production with seeds from Ventura County.

The year 1898 saw some major changes in agriculture in Ventura County. The sugar factory in Oxnard was built, a big barbecue was held on site in February. Between four and five thousand people were in attendance, many taking the newly connected rail line by train. The big feature was a football game between the Lima Beans and the Sugar Beets, captained by Charles Gandolfo and Joe Day. The game ended in a tie, but the county was to win with the introduction of the sugar beet factory.

While lima beans, wheat and barley continued to dominate the county's crop output, the introduction of sugar beets allowed for the supply of the beans to drop and the price of the beans to increase. The crops were complementary to each other. The sugar beet is a deep-rooted plant that attracts nematodes and depletes the soil of nitrogen. The roots of the lima bean house microbes that transfer atmospheric nitrogen into the soil.

The *Ventura Weekly Post and Democrat* reported on July 7, 1899, that Ventura and Santa Barbara Counties combined to plant forty thousand acres in beans, mostly limas, proclaiming the county "the greatest Lima bean producing section of the world."

The *L.A. Times* echoed this claim as the lima bean section of the world in a January 28 article under the heading "Getting Famous."

The total population was just under 300,000, and the county was producing 1,600 carloads of limas, several hundred carloads of citrus, 60 carloads of walnuts, 325 carloads of corn, 400,000 bags of barley and 175,000 bags of wheat. Later in the season, the steamer *Coos Bay* sailed to San Francisco with 1,161 bags of limas while the steamer *Orizaba* sailed with 1,600 bags of limas and 255 bags of dried apricots.

Hauling beans, Camarillo. The town of Camarillo was established with the building of the railroad and train depot in 1899. Many of the businesses from the Springville community were reestablished near the depot. *Jeff Maulhardt.*

The Limoneira Company in Santa Paula planted eighty acres of lima beans with the expectation of one ton per acre. The previous spring, it added two thousand walnut trees to its four-hundred-acre ranch.

Zach Graham threshed beans that came to 2,225 pounds to the acre, about $63 an acre. M.D.L. Todd raised 2,500 pounds of beans on 43 acres. On 28 acres, Hugh Henry on the Colonia raised 26 tons of lima beans that sold for $2,000, with the beans going for $0.04 a pound. Benjamin Wells Dudley had 10 acres in walnuts and 5 acres of a variety of fruit. He planted lima beans between his trees, and they yielded 1,800 pounds per acre. J.F. Cummings had one of the biggest yields on only 10 acres of beans; he produced 3,300 pounds per acre, averaging over $100 an acre. J.S. Harkey in Ojai raised 31 acres of beans that yielded 2,300 pounds an acre. James Ward, a teacher from Montalvo, devoted the majority of his 113 acres to raising lima beans.

The Louis Maulhardt thresher was built by James Fulkerson in 1902. Maulhardt used many of the same men as Callens and Leonard. Among the men in the photograph included Bill Rogers, John Dominquez and Tony Durate. Frank Dutra is second from the right of the group of seven men. *Helen Rolls.*

"Threshing Beans by Electric Light" was the headline from the *Ventura Free Press* on November 18, 1901. The Dixie Thompson Ranch was the first threshing outfit in the country to include the use of electric lights to speed up the threshing time. James Sweat was the ranch manager at this time. Sweat used a dynamo (generator) with direct current at 125 volts and connected directly with a 16-volt horsepower Westinghouse engine to the large engine running the separator. The dynamo was situated on a separate wagon and easily detached. The dynamo had a capacity for sixty lights. This new way of lighting up the working area replaced the old way of burning straw with the unwelcome smoke and inconsistent flare-ups.

The Joseph Lewis eight-thousand-acre Ranch in Camarillo is now home to the State University of Channel Islands. Lewis partnered with Adolfo Camarillo in growing lima beans. *Pleasant Valley Historical Society.*

Also threshing in October 1901 were Frank Petit, Cook and Cannon, Louis Maulhardt, G. Willoughby, P.S. Carr, Joseph Lewis, William Saviers, the Donlon brothers and A. Guillou. The combined daily output was ten thousand sacks a day.

It wasn't until 1902 that the first lima beans were planted in Moorpark. The R.W. Poindexter ranch planted a few hundred acres. However, apricots were better suited for the dryer climate.

September 1902 saw the first of seventeen threshers. Among the machine owner/operators were the Donlon Bros., the Patterson Ranch Co., Albert F. Maulhardt, F. Cook, Cook and Cannon, Dixie Thompson, Willoughby, George Powers, Montalvo Co., Frank Petit, William Saviers, Louis Maulhardt, A.O. Wadleigh, Joe Lewis, Scarlett and Lewis, Hill Bros. and M.V. Carr.

In 1903, Southern California produced 755,000 sacks of lima beans. Ventura County produced 600,000 sacks, Santa Monica 120,000 and Santa Ana 35,000 sacks.

For a short time, Los Angeles County gave Ventura County a run for the title of lima bean capital of the world. In the area that became Beverly Hills, the Hammel and Denker ranch covered 2,400 acres, and the majority was planted to lima beans in 1904. Willoughby Brothers, from Ventura County, farmed 1,300 acres of this land and was considered one of the most extensive bean farmers in the country. Others growing beans in the area included Dozier Lewis, also from Ventura County, 300 acres; Balcom & Co, 300 acres; and a Mr. Shanks, 2,050 acres. On the Wolfskill track, 1,500 acres were farmed, with the majority going to Barnard and Silva.

Oswald, Saviers and the Willoughby Brothers were doing most of the threshing in Los Angeles County. The latter ran the biggest bean threshing outfit with a machine that used a sixty-inch cylinder with a capacity for two thousand sacks a day.

Willoughby Brothers also farmed a portion of the Dixie Thompson Ranch. In 1904, James Swett was serving as the manager of the ranch, and it was considered the largest bean ranch in the world. On September 14, Swett sent President Roosevelt the first sack from the ranch, the earliest the beans had been harvested up to this time. The outfit would thresh 2,500 bags of beans per day before finishing at an expected 16,000 sacks, down from the 21,000 the year before.

In 1906, Joseph F. Lewis purchased 8,200 acres of the Guadalasca Rancho from Adolfo Camarillo. Lewis had been farming lima beans since he was a boy growing up on his father's farm in Carpinteria. He relocated to Camarillo in Ventura County in 1889 and leased land from the Camarillo family. He introduced the Lewis Lima, or Common Lima, to Ventura County. Though he continued farming in the Montalvo area during the 1890s, Lewis returned to Camarillo in 1901 and formed a partnership with Adolfo Camarillo. Lewis later completed a business block in Camarillo in 1816, located not far from the train station. The building remains in use today and is home to a restaurant and bar, Twisted Oaks Tavern. Lewis also helped organize the Farmers Bank of Camarillo.

Bean harvesters at work in September 1908 included Petit & Edwards, War & Cannon, Frank Cook, Joe Lewis, Gill Bros., Mart Carr, Donlon Bros., Dunn & Chrisman, Nauman Bros., Louis Maulhardt, Thermal Belt Threshing Co., R.C. Sudden, O.A. Wadleigh, Frank Petit, Patterson Ranch Co., J.B. Dawley and George S. Power.

A reformed Lima Bean Growers Association was organized in 1910 with its principal place of business in Oxnard. The association included growers from Ventura, Santa Paula, Santa Barbara, Los Angeles and Orange Counties. The association's primary objective was to protect the industry from being manipulated by buyers and speculators. The other goal was to guarantee the shipment of the cleanest and best-prepared product. Up to this time, the East Coast bean market had been controlled by the J.K. Armsby Company, and the California growers felt Armsby

was spreading falsehoods about the amount of beans available and thus manipulating the market to his advantage. The articles were filed in May 1910, and early directors included T.G. Gabbert, Hiram K. Snow, Joseph McGrath and President Charles Donlon from Oxnard; R.G. Edwards, George C. Power, D.F. Sheldon and John Darling of Saticoy; Clarence Chrisman, Ventura; F.A. Snyder, Somis; and Adolfo Camarillo, Camarillo.

Bean production was growing each year, depending on the weather. The lowest total for the first decade was in 1902, which produced 78,016,000 pounds. The largest yield was the 1909 crop at 202,400,000 pounds. Twelve-month records for lima beans grown of thirty-five thousand acres totaled 1.25 million sacks and 90 million pounds. Oxnard was growing three-fourths of the world's bean crop.[35]

This is the Edwards and Petit threshing outfit circa 1914. Roger Edwards of Saticoy teamed up with several owners including John Petit and later Frank Pidduck. Frank Eastman was the main operator and Cleve Wiltfong, mechanic, for the Edwards Petit thresher. *Ayers Family Archives.*

In 1911, lima bean production almost doubled to 60,000 acres and 900,000 sacks. Sugar beets accounted for 15,000 acres, producing 187,000 tons of beets. Lemons were up to 500 acres, and the claim of being the largest-bearing orchards in the world was also applied to citrus from the county. English walnuts were the fourth-largest crop, producing 3 million pounds.

An article titled "Men Who Raise Beans and Who Know Beans" provided information about several important lima bean growers, including Adolfo

Camarillo, who at this time was director of the Lima Bean Association as well as supervisor for the Second District and one of the largest bean growers in the county. Thomas Bell was from El Rio, what today would be Oxnard, off Rice Avenue. He was a former supervisor and owner of one of the finest farms in the county. Charles Donlon was the Hueneme and Oxnard representative for the Bean Growers Association. Along with his brothers, the Donlons represented over one thousand acres of lima beans.

Top: Hauling beets, Camarillo circa 1910. Among the early lima bean farmers in Camarillo at this time included Arneill, Benn, Camarillo, Cawleti, Coultas, Crowley, Daily, Dunn, Flynn, Fulton, Gill, Gisler, Glenn, Haigh, Hartman, Helm, Hughes, Hunt, Lewis, Maulhardt, McCormick, Riggs, Romero, Russell, Saviers, Scholle, Spencler, Souza, Suytar, Tico, Wadleigh, Wallace, Willard, Wood. *Pleasant Valley Historical Society*.

Bottom: This image by J.M Waterman of the Lima Bean Growers Association shows the right portion of a panoramic of the Gill Brothers bean threshing outfit circa 1916. *Pleasant Valley Historical Society, courtesy Bill Milligan.*

F.A. Snyder was manager of the Las Posas Rancho that belonged to Thomas Bard, two thousand acres of which were in lima beans; Snyder owned four hundred. Ashby Vickers was from the Del Norte Section and farmed two hundred acres in beans.

The population of Ventura was five thousand, while Oxnard was home to three thousand, followed by Santa Paula with two thousand residents. In describing Oxnard, Secretary of the Board of Trade J.R. Gabbert stretched the title to "The Biggest Little City on the Coast" in an article that wound up in *Out West* magazine, May 1912.

Lima beans can also lead to romance, as evidenced by the union of Thomas Bard Jr. and Anne Carolyn Dallavo. The junior Bard was running his father's eight-hundred-acre Somis property, where he was growing lima beans. He was in Oxnard to procure his bean seed for the season when he spied "a tall, graceful girl with blue eyes and dark hair and a pretty face walking down the street."[36] He noticed her checking into the Oxnard Hotel and decided to stay for dinner and search out an introduction. Once acquainted, Bard shared his enthusiasm for his upcoming bean prospects and intrigued the young lady. Miss Dallavo was employed by the Donlon brothers. They soon became engaged, and it was her wish to get married in her home state of Michigan. Due to the impending bean planting season, they decided to elope to Bakersfield for a quiet wedding and return in time to tend to his beans.

The Ventura County Courthouse was completed in 1913. The Neoclassical building was designed by the renowned architect A.C. Martin, who had a connection to the area: he was married to Carrie Borchard, granddaughter of Christian Borchard, who planted the first commercial crop in 1867. This connection led to many designing opportunities in Ventura County, and the courthouse in Ventura proved to be an architectural treasure that is listed on the National Register of Historic Places. Another interesting connection to agriculture is Martin's use of lima bean bouquets for the bronze entry gates, signifying the importance of the crop to the area.

The year 1914 saw some of the same threshing operators, with the addition of several new threshermen. Among the outfits working the bean fields included the Gill brothers, who started in the Santa Susana region and worked their way through Simi, Somis, Camarillo and Oxnard. Ramie Callens threshed the Hill Ranch in the Santa Rosa Valley section. The Petit machine worked the Ed Petit Ranch near Somis, and Henry Maulhardt's machine worked the fields of Camarillo.

The Valentine & Arneill outfit started on the Will Arneill Ranch, and Ward & Cannon worked the Springville area, owned by the American Beet Sugar Company.

Many fields produced some of their best yields. Thomas McCormick averaged thirty sacks per acre. Charles J. Daily averaged thirty-five sacks an acre, up fifteen sacks an acre. Joe Olivas increased production by three hundred sacks on a 50-acre field. Ed Barnard had a good showing for his 760 acres. Thomas Steele, who ran the Bean Threshing Co.'s machine, turned out eighteen thousand sacks for the Camarillo Ranch. The Ferro Company reached five thousand sacks on the Del Norte Ranch. C.C. Perkins harvested 500 acres, averaging twenty-four sacks an acre.

A new era of development for the industry and a new commercial outlet came about with the introduction of canning green limas. J.M. Waterman of the Lima Bean Growers Association had the first of several canneries built in Sawtelle, in West Lost Angeles County, with a capacity of producing fifty thousand cans a day.

Shipley Warehouse, Santa Paula. Shipley began working in the banking business for A. Levy in Hueneme and by 1907 had opened a general commission business in Santa Paula. *Craig Held.*

The crew of John C. Hartman planting beans at the foot of the Conejo Grade on land rented from Camarillo. Hartman arrived 1874 with his mother, who later married John Young Saviers. *Museum of Ventura County, photograph 4781.*

By 1915, the county was growing 67,000 acres in lima beans, with 120,000 acres within the state. However, participation the Lima Bean Growers Association was down. Without a commitment of 50,000 acres, the association took a gamble and decided to suspend business in June 1915, leaving the individual grower to fight for a deal with brokers. While the association's operations were suspended for the year, President Charles Donlon pledged to not dissolve the organization.

While 1914 was a banner year, production was down in 1915 from 10 to 25 percent in some areas. However, Bert Culbert was only three sacks shy of the previous year, and Mrs. Will Arneill came within ten sacks short. F.A. Snyder was also close to the previous year's output by coming up short only four sacks. Yet, the Hill ranch came eight hundred sacks shy of the previous mark.

Those threshing beans in September 1915 included John Petit, who threshed the Gabe Gisler ranch in Springville; Frank Petit, on the Charles Daily Ranch; Gill Bros., on the Morris Cohn place; Donlon Bros., on the Las Posas; Dan Emmett, on the upper Las Posas; Callens Leonard, on the Callens ranch; Patterson Ranch Co. in Simi; Cook and Valentine with Harry Haydock in the Saticoy section; the Ward machine at Pat Flynn's; and Frank Wadleigh and Jon Dawley were also threshing beans at this time.

The gamble to wait worked. By the end of the year, the association had been reorganized, with each district creating its own association under the umbrella of the Lima Bean Growers charter. However, it was an expensive lesson for the growers, as the market used the lack of unity to clip off a dollar a pound, costing the growers $1 million.[37]

One of the other battles the association faced was protecting the lima bean from beans grown in other parts of the world that claimed to be limas. Imported beans such as Manchurian, Korean or Madagascar beans were determined to be of a common variety of beans, *Phaseolus vulgaris*, different that the lima bean species, *Phaseolus lunatus*. The decision came from the Bureau of Chemistry under the Food and Drugs Board. This decision protected the quality of beans labeled limas as well as the price of the beans. However, this did not take the Madagascar beans off the market, and they would be a threat to the sale of beans for years to come.

President Wilson became the next (and not last) U.S. president to receive a shipment of lima beans when Simon Cohn sent a sack in 1916.

The war years of 1917 and 1918 proved profitable for most bean growers. There was a need to feed the troops, and beans offered a high protein

Patrick Flynn sitting on stacked beans and his son George Flynn, Camarillo. Brothers Michael and Martin Flynn were also bean farmers. The Flynn family emigrated from Ireland in 1878. *Mary Caroline Chunn.*

Charles Lichau (*middle*) and crew on the Lloyd Butler Ranch, Del Norte Rancho, circa 1919. Lichau also farmed the Gordon Ranch, Oxnard. *Chuck Covarrubias.*

and carbohydrate content food with a low spoilage rate. The amount of acreage grown in beans in California almost doubled from 1916 to 1917 to 558,000 acres.

However, the biggest surprise for most farmers was when they were unable to put their beans on the market. On March 31, 1917, the *Morning Free Press* announced: "GOVERNMENT SEIZES LIMA BEANS OF COUNTY GROWERS."

Several lima bean growers in Ventura County received orders for delivery at once from the payment master general of the navy directing the farmers to ship their beans to Boston. Non-association member Simon Cohn of El Rio was ordered to ship 6,000 bags. James McLaughlin was to send 7,800 bags. The Lima Bean Growers Association also received an order. The growers were promised a "fair and just profit." However, this eliminated the choice of holding on to the beans and selling during the spring, when prices usually peaked.

A few weeks after sending in their orders, a soldier from Ventura, Jimmy Hollingsworth, who was stationed at Waco, Texas, wrote to a friend in Ventura that he was pleasantly surprised to be served lima beans, which made him homesick.

Briggs School near Santa Paula did its part for the war. After the farmers harvested the beans, the students formed two teams, one boys and one girls, to glean the fields. The girls won and were able to gather eighty dollars in beans, which they turned over to the Red Cross, and paid the membership fees for all the pupils in the school.

By September, the sacks started coming into the warehouses. Robert Beardsley from the Pleasant Valley district was the first rancher to get in seven hundred one-hundred-pound sacks. Thomas McCormick's ranch saw his production drop 15 percent, and Martin Flynn's crop was down 20 percent. Thomas and James McLaughlin were down two sacks per acre. The Ventura District was down 10 percent. Even the Irvine District in Orange County was down 20 percent for the year. However, Thomas Richardson, who farmed the Schiappa-Pietra ranch, was one of the few who reported a gain in beans per acre. J.R. Callens installed electric lighting on his bean thresher, saving the burning of bean straw to light the nighttime activities.

The year 1918 was a peak for lima bean production. Nearly 1.8 million bags were gathered. The next ten years would see a drop in production with the increased planting of citrus and walnuts. While the majority of beans required no irrigation beyond Mother Nature, more and more fields were relying on irrigation, and by this time, two-thirds of the beans were under irrigation. This also allowed more areas to begin growing limas, including Newbury Park and the Conejo area. Casper Borchard Jr. was one of few farmers to plant lima beans in Newbury Park, adjusting his thresher to handle threshing the crop.

On September 15, Gus Naumann delivered the first crop of the season to the Hueneme warehouse from his Ocean View ranch.

The war also had an effect on German Americans. Many of the early farming families in Oxnard were of German descent. Their influence was prominent in building the parochial schools, churches and hospital. In fact, the first sermon at the Santa Clara Chapel back in 1878 was in German. However, in January 1918, the board of trustees for the Oxnard High School district unanimously voted to exclude the study of German. Other parts of the county were also affected. The town of Nordhoff was officially changed to Ojai. A hamburger became a liberty sandwich. A hot dog was called a liberty sausage. While the name changes weren't permanent, they were reapplied during the next world war.

The Mexican population of Oxnard was also affected by the war. The local paper reported that estimates of Mexican residents leaving ranged from fifty to one hundred and Police Chief Murray believed up to six hundred Mexicans returned to Mexico. The number of families living in the Enterprise Street area dropped from twelve to four. Reasons for leaving

Farel Ayers captured this north-facing image of bean threshing just west of Santa Paula. *Ayer Family Archives.*

ranged from fear of the draft and the rumor of free land offered by President Carranza of Mexico.[38]

The year 1918 also saw an investment of farming as another way to support the war effort. The more efficient the fieldwork, the more productive the output. H.H. Eastwood was the sales agent for Holt Caterpillar, and by purchasing these tractors, a farmer would be able to replace the work of 22 horses as well as work night and day. With the purchase of thirty-six tractors, 396 horses became available for war work.

Among the farmers who purchased a Caterpillar tractor for $4,700 each included John Lloyd Butler, Adolfo Camarillo, Joe Baptiste, Diedrich Company, George Henry, Mrs. Francisco Suytar, Robert Beardsley, Frank Gilser, Mike Flynn, the Barr Brothers, James Horton, Corey and Schwedhelm, McGrath Estate, H.H. Eastwood, James Ward and Enoch Waters.

In 1919, the Lima Bean Growers Association decided it was time to advertise nationally. A trademark was adopted to distinguish their beans from other beans. The trademark consisted of a map of California with the words "California Seaside Lima Beans" and would be used for regular lima beans. For smaller beans, the use of "Baby Limas" was substituted. Soon, ads began appearing in the *Saturday Evening Post* and other national magazines. The association recognized that branding had made other products—Sunkist oranges, Sun Maid raisins and Quaker Oats—household names.

To coincide with the new campaign offering ads and recipes, two-pound bags were offered for the first time. Previously, beans were sold in eighty- to one-hundred-pound bags. The Saticoy Warehouse became the first to ever ship out two-pound packs. The sacks were packed in forty bags to a case. By March 1920, the beans were shipped out to all the major stores with new displays.

For the fall season of 1920, Thomas McCormick of Camarillo was among the first to have his beans threshed with the Daily Bros. doing the work. His crop was 10 percent better than the previous year. At this time, threshing outfits were paid $1.25 per sack.

The following year, 1921, offered a glimpse in proceeds in Ventura County. Lima beans produced $2,669,100 in sales—over twice the amount of sugar beets, which brought in $1,096,801, but less than lemons, which brought in $3,721,800. Other top crops included walnuts at $1,800,000 and oranges—navel, Valencia and miscellaneous—at $1,500,000. Apricots bought in nearly $1,000,000.

Production of lima beans almost doubled the following year, from 43.4 million pounds of lima beans in 1922 to 70.8 million pounds of limas in 1923, surpassing lemons by $1,000,000 in proceeds with $5,125,000. Baby limas also made an appearance in the county with 250,000 pounds grown.

Walter Argabrite was crowned champion lima bean grower in the Mound District in 1924 when he averaged thirty-three sacks an acre. Coming in a close second was Albert Thille, who averaged thirty-two sacks per acre. Thille planted his crop in four separate plots to test a variety of seed he'd been propagating for some time.

In 1925, the county produced fifty million tons of lima beans and almost two million tons of baby limas, which sold at $0.105 per pound. The production grew to eight million tons but sold at only $0.06 a pound. This prompted the lima bean growers to plant sugar beets to reduce to abundance of beans in the market and allow the price to go back up. This would take a few years to catch up.

The D. McGrath Estate Company produced sixteen sacks per acre on 255 acres on their Gonzales Road property and almost as well on the Hugo McGrath Ranch in Montalvo. The McGraths also threshed Tom McCormick's 100-acre ranch off Ditch Road (today Rose Avenue) for a total of 1,200 sacks.

John Arneill threshed 2,337 sacks on one hundred acres; Albert Noble got 21 sacks an acre; and John Spencler threshed 1,987 sacks from ninety-five acres or 20 sacks an acre. Wendell Daily got 1,674 sacks off eighty acres.

John K. Thille arrived in 1889 and settled in Santa Paula. In 1926, the Albert Thille crew set a season record for producing 1,827 sacks in one day. The family eventually switched to avocados, lemons and oranges and became one of the founders of Calavo Growers. *Pleasant Valley Historical Society, courtesy Bill Milligan.*

Bert Culbert produced 21 sacks an acre, and T.F. McFarland had one of his best crops as well.

Enoch Waters from Camarillo threshed fifty thousand sacks of lima beans in forty-two days with the Waters-Hitch threshing machine. Waters used fifty-two men and needed to thresh nine hundred sacks a day to pay expenses.

Records for bean production were being broken almost yearly because of improved farming practices. In April 1926, Albert Thille completed installing irrigation to his fields, which allowed time to time the water distribution. The investment paid off with a large harvest. Thille even set a record of 1,827 sacks in a one day of bagging.

Over on the Cloyne Ranch near Oxnard, Floyd Tyler and Peter Fournier used their new thresher to harvest lima beans.

Even though the country was in the throes of Prohibition, many cities still had a section of town where alcohol and gambling thrived. Oxnard had an area off A Street labeled China Alley named for its many Chinese establishments that offered more than a meal and or commerce. For the owners of the threshing machines, this proved to be a problem if their operations were interrupted during harvesting season. Rain and fog could halt operations until the warm weather returned, and in the meantime, the crew had idle time. The *Press Courier* had a suggestion for lawmakers during these times, as evidenced in this September 17, 1927 headline: "Temperance Union Should Prohibit Fog, Causes Drunkenness."

The article pointed out the workmen took their money, came into town and proceeded to have a "hilarious change from the heavy field work." Many arrests were made for intoxication.

Threshing outfits in the Camarillo district in September 1927 included Jim Gill, Bob Lefever, Urban Underwood, Joe Terry, Smith and Mahan, Joe Terry, Daily Bros., Charles Donlon and Gill & Wucherpfennig. Lima bean production in Ventura County was up to sixty-three thousand acres, while Orange County was up to forty-five thousand acres and San Fernando planted over ten thousand acres.

In 1928, Ventura County grew lima beans on 42,421 acres; Orange County, 23,183 acres; and Santa Barbara County at 6,160 acres. Beans were also grown in San Diego, Los Angeles and King City for a total of 78,693 acres in the state.

In Camarillo, bean planting began as early as April, with John Arneill setting out his seeds, as did the Daily Brothers, Mrs. Pat Flynn, Lorenzo Ward and George Doty.

The end of the decade was also the end of the lead in returns for lima beans. Regular limas brought in $6,350,000, while baby limas added another $108,050. Lemons were a close second at $5,759,200. Walnuts were third with almost $3 million, with hay fourth and sugar beets sixth.

The year 1930 saw lemons take and hold the lead as the top crop in Ventura County for the next seven decades before being replaced by strawberries as the leading crop in 1999. However, Ventura County was still raising more lima beans than any other place in the world. Over fifty-four thousand acres were still being planted and brought in nearly $7 million during these early Depression-era times.

Test plots to improve the bean quality and production with the help of University of California agronomy division were underway in the county in 1930. The plots were located at the Albert Noble ranch in Camarillo and the Albert Thille ranch in the Mound District, The plots consisted of two acres, and the planting would take place at five different times, with the first planting on May 6.

Many other areas beyond Ventura County have experimented with growing lima beans. In 1930, Abner C. Hibbits, farming a few miles east of Lompoc, revealed that he had performed a series of selective seeding, cultivation, irrigation and seasonal plantings of lima beans over a four-year period. A series of plots was set up, and the results were tallied and presented to the

Santa Barbara Farm Bureau. The results were shared with other Lompoc farmers, and while Hibbits eventually turned to growing walnuts, his research helped Lompoc farmers gain a rebirth in growing lima beans. His son Charles took this knowledge with him when he relocated to Camarillo and continued growing lima beans and eventually operated five threshing machines.

Lima beans to the rescue! On March 10, 1933, a 6.4 earthquake hit Long Beach, killing 120 people, injuring over 500 and causing $50 million in damages. Within a few days, the residents of Camarillo gathered donations of lima beans and other provisions for the food kitchen in Long Beach. Among those who donated beans included the Daily brothers, Adolfo Camarillo, Reg Newman, A. Cawelti, Marilyn Flynn, F.M. Aggen, Wendell Daily, Thomas Bard, Robert Milligan and Charles Pope. The trucks to transport the goods were provided by Adolfo Camarillo.

The communities of Oxnard, Ventura, Santa Paula, Fillmore and Simi also sent lima beans and other relief items to the earthquake victims.

Among the Somis and Camarillo district ranchers who began their threshing operations in September 1938 were Robert Lefever, Urban Underwood, Enoch Waters, Robert Nelson and Albert Wucherpfennig.

The end of the 1930s saw lemons take a commanding lead in crop returns, bringing in nearly $7 million. Valencias improved to over $4 million. Dry limas, baby limas and seed beans edged out walnuts with $2.3 million. Beans as a total declined in number each year starting in 1936, when beans topped $4 million.

The year 1940 was a big one for lima bean promotion. However, it was also a year that the surplus of the previous four years reached a record high. A committee headed by Hugh Sellers, manager of the J.C. Penny Co. in Oxnard, presided over a committee of businessmen and city officials to come up with a plan to solve the problem. The plan was for a nationwide "blitzkrieg" from January 16 to January 23, 1941. Sellers claimed the overstock "is the problem of every citizen of Ventura County and we must show enthusiasm for lima beans if we expect the nation to do so."[39]

The National Lima Bean Week was approved. The Lima Bean Growers Association sent a quantity of beans to President Roosevelt as part of National Lima Bean Week. The association worked with the Ventura County Chamber of Commerce to promote a National Bean Week starting on January 16. Over three thousand chain food stores featured beans all week, and stickers were used on all the diners of Southern Pacific trains traveling from Oregon to New Orleans. In Ventura County, over eighty establishments offered displays of beans.

Directors of the Lima Bean Association circa 1940s. Adolfo Camarillo in pictured front row, middle. The direction of the lima bean industry was about to change with the introduction of flash freezing by Birds Eye and the availability of home freezers. More farmers began planting the Fordhook green limas. *Robert Louis Maulhardt.*

This same month, a committee of five men, including R.L. Churchill, manager of the California Lima Bean Association, and Camarillo rancher John Arneill, was in charge of arranging seventy thousand bags of large and standard limas for sale to the federal surplus marketing administration.

In 1941, a new lima bean was announced. Through the efforts of W.W. Mackie, a University of California agronomist, and with the support of the Ventura County Farm Bureau and the Camarillo State Hospital, the five-year experiment to improve the lima bean was complete. The new "Ventura" lima bean was known as No. 7402 and came about after crossing a variety of lima bean seeds that ended with this new variety that grows a more uniform plant with a vigorous vine with wide climatic adaptation—plus it is superior in quality for canning and quick freezing. The seeds were made available for planting in 1942 and sold though the California Lima Bean Association. The year 1942 saw the introductions of the first paper sacks to save on burlap needed for the war effort. The new sacks were made up of five plys of paper sewed with an electronic sewing machine.

During World War II, the lima bean came to the rescue again, this time as one of twelve meals in a case of the C-Rations for the troops. The meal came in a twelve-ounce tin plate can that opened with a key. The limas were combined with a piece of salty ham that contained 3,700 calories. As part of the C-Rats, it earned several names, including Hammy Limas, Ham & Lifers, Ham and Claymores and Ham and Mother———. For many, it was an unpopular meal. The meal stuck around until the Vietnam War and became universally hated. However, in fairness to the lima beans, any food packed with salted pork and grease would taste bad.

Other changes came to the lima bean industry during this time. While Ventura County was the leading producer of limas in California, Orange County and specifically the Irvine Ranch saw changes to the area that knocked them out of the lima bean competition. In 1942, the lima bean fields of the Irvine Ranch were viewed as a perfect location for a Marine Corps air base. Irvine Ranch alone farmed 17,000 acres of lima beans. By 1947, lima bean acreage in Orange County was down to 27,715 acres. Ten years later there were barely 20,000 acres, and within thirty years of the construction of the air base, the lima bean crops were down to 831 acres.

By 1945, the Fordhook 242 improved lima bean had been introduced. The bush plant offered a wider spreading plant for more foliage, an earlier

Bob Pfeiler planting daughters instead of beans. Bob became the founder of the Ventura County Agriculture Museum in Santa Paula after years of collection farm equipment throughout the county. *Robert Pfeiler.*

yield and heavier yield. This would become the most popular seed for the next seventy-five years.

In 1946, Thornhill Brooke died at his residence in Chicago. This left his California property without management. The 38,593-acre Rancho Guadalasca passed through several hands, starting with Ysabel Yorba in 1836, and in 1880, the rancho ended up in the possession of Lord William and Lady Frances Broome. Frances ended up with one-third of the rancho after her husband died. After she passed away in 1921, her son Thornhill bought out his siblings and oversaw the ranch from Chicago with occasional visits to the property. After his passing in 1946, his urban-born and raised son John Spoor Broome took over the ranch.

John Spoor Broome, known as Jack, was a pilot. He was a flight supervisor during World War II and then worked for American Airlines as part of the Air Transport Command. After getting married in July 1946, the couple made the Rancho Guadalasca their new home.

While lima beans had been grown on the expansive Broome Ranch for years, Jack had never planted a seed before. He credits farmers John Newman, Andy Callens and Mike Vujovich with helping him take over the ranch operations. In a 2003 interview, Jack gave further credit to Jim Dowd, Ed Carty and Eddie Maulhardt in helping him learn the farming business. Eddie Maulhardt was leasing five hundred acres from the Broome estate to grow lima beans at the time Jack relocated to the area. These men became Jack's friends while he adjusted to finding a way to keep the large acreage. "I had good friends who took me by the hand and saved it."[40]

Broome learned to grow lima beans very well. He would serve on several boards, including the Lima Bean Advisor Group in 1959, along with Henry Borchard and Harold Bell. Broome would later become a major contributor to California State University Channel Island, where the John Spoor Broome Library opened in 2008.

The Farm Bureau reported in 1946 that there was an increased demand for frozen fruits. For the first time, green lima beans were threshed in the county. This represented the fourth harvesting method in the history of lima beans, the first being the tramping out of the beans followed by the stationary thresher and evolving into the pickup-type thresher that raveled up the cut beans on wind rows. This fourth method, applied to the green limas used for freezing, used a thresher called a viner. After the beans were cut, instead of being left to dry, the green vine was fed into the viner machine and entered into a large centrifuge where paddles beat the vines until the pods opened and the beans fell into a chute (more info in Threshers chapter).

By the end of the year 1946, Oxnard saw the construction of two plants. At a cost of $300,000, the Stokely–Van Camp packinghouse joined forces with Union Ice Company on its property located at North Harrison Avenue and Third Street. In addition to packing lima beans, the warehouse handled peas, carrots, cauliflower, broccoli, lettuce, orange and lemon juice and spinach. The plant ran two eight-hours shifts with up to 120 workers per shift. The company also constructed twenty-four threshing machines used for harvesting the green lima beans.

Ventura Farms Frozen Foods invested $400,000 for its processing plant along Fifth Street in Oxnard next to the railroad tracks on land purchased from J.T. Diaz. The idea came from Thomas Leonard after he heard a speech by Hubert Dalton from the Farm Bureau about the studies of frozen food plants in the state. Birds Eye was the first to offer quick-freeze frozen foods in the 1920s, and by the 1940s, the concept of offering easier preparation to feed the family began taking hold. Leonard began a conversation with Dalton as well as Ernest Borchard and Jack C. Miller.

Leonard and Borchard were joined by R.A. Farrell, Peter Fox, Thomas Daily and Ellen Leonard to incorporate. William Salter came on board as the general manager, and plans for the building were designed by well-known architect Roy Wilson. The streamlined, state-of-the-art building was complete by November 1, 1948, and included eighteen thousand square

Built in 1948, the Pleasant Valley Lima Bean Growers and Warehouse Association represented the largest bean warehouse in the world for nearly fifty years. *Frank Naumann.*

Leo Gisler loading sacks of limas off Gonzales Road, Oxnard, circa 1950s. Gisler moved to Porterville, California, in 1971 and continued farming into his nineties. *Chuck Covarrubias.*

feet with a cold storage that held five hundred tons of frozen foods. Initial employment was two hundred women and seventy-five men.

The year 1948 saw the construction of a warehouse for the Pleasant Valley Lima Bean Growers and Warehouse Association, located between Camarillo and Oxnard at the intersection of Pleasant Valley Road and East Fifth Street. The cost was $300,000, and the facility had a capacity for 200,000 tons of beans. It became the largest lima bean warehouse in the world. Charles "Mike" Carr, formally the manager of the Hueneme Warf and Warehouse Company, was appointed the manager of the new warehouse. The board of directors for the association included Glynn Chase, president; Herbert Lyttle, vice president; Robert Friedrich, secretary-treasurer; Don Woolsey; Harold Bell; and Reg Newman.

The first load of beans came on September 14, 1948, at 3:00 p.m. from Jake Immel of Santa Rosa Valley in a truck driven by Jack Pitts and threshed by Harold Bell. Immel had his name and handprint imprinted in fresh concrete at the warehouse. J.R. Silva came in a close second.

The warehouse coincided with the new method of handling the beans. No longer would farmers need to bundle the beans into burlap sacks before they were shipped. The new method of bulk handling skips the sewing, handling and shipping to the warehouse. In bulk handling, the beans pass through the thresher and separator and are put right into a truck for shipping directly to the warehouse. This eliminated the three to four sewers as well as the crew who follow the thresher and toss the sacks in the trucks. Plus, the beans don't have to be left out in the field to spoil or be stolen. Once at the warehouse, the beans could be packed into one- and two-pound bags.

By 1949, forty million pounds of lima beans were stored at the Pleasant Valley Lima Bean Warehouse, valued at $7 million. By storing the beans in the farmers-owned warehouse, the growers saved $0.65 off each one-hundred-pound bag. The thirty-eight thousand acres of lima beans grown by the 140 growers represented half of the beans grown in the world, and the warehouse stored one-third of the world's supply.

The Fordhook green lima bean production was on the rise. Starting in 1945, California packaged a little more than seven million pounds of Fordhook lima beans. By 1949, the amount had risen to thirty-five million pounds. There were seventeen new frozen processing plants in the state. The acreage dedicated to growing the green lima beans increased from four thousand acres in the state in 1945 to twenty thousand acres in 1949. However, in the South Coast, which includes Ventura County, the first Fordhook lima beans were not planted until 1946, with less than three million pounds produced. By 1949, the South Coast produced nearly ten million pounds, with that number to triple in the next decade.

The 1950s saw continued growth of the lima bean industry in the county. The warehouses in Saticoy, El Rio and Pleasant Valley saw record numbers for most of the decade. In November 1952, the Pleasant Valley Lima Bean Growers Association warehouse saw a new all-time record set for handling beans. Taking advantage of the east winds that helped dry out the beans, a total of thirty-six thousand bags or 3.6 million pounds of beans were hauled into the warehouse in a twenty-four-hour period. The totals were lower for the other two warehouses but still brisk at ten thousand bags in Saticoy and seven thousand bags in El Rio. At this time, there were thirty-one thousand acres in beans in the county.

While Ventura County was number 1 in production of lima beans in the United States, the song "Lima Bean" by Eddie Ware is a contender for the first rock-and-roll song. Recorded on January 23, 1951, the song predates the census's first rock-and-roll recorded, "Rocket 88" by Jackie Brenston and Jis Delta Cats, which was recorded March 5, 1951. However, the Chess label out of Chicago issued Brenston's song in April, while Ware's song was released a month later in May 1951. Both songs featured an aggressive rhythm and blues tempo with an amplified guitar line that later became associated with rock-and-roll.

Ware's love of lima beans came from his upbringing in Alabama, and he later moved to Chicago, where he recorded his love for the legume. Ware played piano for blues legends Little Walter and Jimmy Reed. In between a session with Reed, Ware laid down the catchy and fun R&B tune. The song "Lima Bean" became a minor hit for the Chess label but still hits home for its timeless rhythm.

While neither of these songs were played at the Lima Bean Festival sponsored by the Camarillo Chamber of Commerce in 1954, there was still plenty of music, dance and activities. The event evolved into Camarillo's Ranchero Days Festival and today's Camarillo Fiesta.

However, a slow decline began to occur as more and more farmland was being taken up by new subdivisions and more competitive crops. By 1953, the acreage was down to 26,000; 1956, 22,000 acres; 1957, 18,700 acres; 1959, 16,000 acres; 1960, 13,200 acres. However, the acreage planted to Fordhook lima beans for freezing increased from 100 acres in 1945 to 15,000 acres by 1961.

The price for lima beans during this decade ranged from $10 to $12 per one hundred pounds, though with the decline in the area in production, the price by 1960 was up to $17. On the production side, lima bean production was hitting its stride in 1954. Over one thousand field and factory workers were in the middle of a busy fifty-day bean harvest season. Lima beans grown for Oxnard Frozen Foods and Stokely–Van Camp were the county's ninth-most valuable crop at $3.5 million grown on eleven thousand acres by seventy-five county farmers.

General Foods Corp. announced in 1956 it would purchase a ten-acre parcel off Third Street near the railroad tracks to build a $1 million quick frozen food plant. An updated article put the plant's construction in the fall of 1958.

Ventura Farms Frozen Foods was sold in 1959 for $1.4 million to a co-op of farmers headed by John F. Dullam under the name of Oxnard Frozen Foods. Joining Dullam were Frank and John Vujovich, John Laubacher, Steve Laubacher, John Kellner, A.A. Milligan and Milton Diedrich.

Officers included Ernest Borchard, president; Richard Bard, vice president; Thomas Daily, secretary; and H.E. Grether, Thomas Leonard, Fred Snodgrass, G.R. McComb Jr., Robert Naumann and A.A. Milligan, directors.

The new co-op announced it would process in excess of twenty-five million pounds of green lima beans. Approximately seventy-five growers from the county would be participating, and they would be taking over the Ventura Farms accounts as well as adding the Birds Eye division of General Foods.

The decade ended with dry lima bean production down to 8,976 acres after starting the decade at almost 17,000 acres. Green beans surpassed dry lima beans with 10,000 acres in production. Lemons still topped the list with 22,000 acres bringing in $54 million followed by Valencia oranges a far second at $17 million. Strawberries were grown on only 915 acres yet still brought in $9 million. Avocados brought in $3 million grown on 3,000 acres. Walnuts saw the biggest drop-off in production, starting the decade at 9,741 acres and ending the decade at 3,405 acres. The industry was constantly at war with walnut crown rot and other diseases.

Despite the fact that the county had been growing lima beans for nearly eighty years, improving the lima bean was always a concern for the best crop and fattest profits. The University of California at Davis worked with the Green Lima Bean Association in 1962. They conducted a series of experiments on the Frank McGrath Ranch off Gonzales Road by planting six different Fordhook seeds to learn which would produce the greenest, tenderest and tastiest product. The results were shared with the local farmers in the coming years.

Frank Vujovich was elected president of the Oxnard Frozen Foods Cooperation in 1963. Vujovich was part owner of Coastal Valley Canning and a partner in Santa Clara Produce. John Kellner was elected vice president, and Thomas Brucker was elected as a director.

Oxnard Frozen Foods Cooperative was also working on improving the industry by experimenting with an improved mechanical picker. Field boss Gino Lorenzi revealed that the new picker was similar to the string bean picker that had been in use for several years.

In 1965, Lorenzi announced that the green Fordhook limas were of "excellent quality," but the yield was slightly down. At this time, Oxnard Frozen Foods Cooperative was the world's largest packer of frozen Fordhook lima beans. The company also processed broccoli, cauliflower, baby limas, peas and peppers. The co-op was owned by seventy-five growers with officers Mike Vujovich, president; Thomas Brucker, vice president; John Laubacher, secretary; Raymond Swift, treasurer; and David Petit, John Kellner, Joseph Terry, Robert Beardsley and A.A. Milligan, directors. George Rees was the general manager.

The co-op also introduced the mobile viner, FMC LV, which cut down the time between picking and processing and eliminated the need for hauling the vines and beans to a separate viner station before processing.

The dry lima bean harvest was also down from fifteen thousand acres in 1964 to ten thousand in 1965.

The California Bean Growers Association was still headquartered in Oxnard, nearly fifty years since first incorporating here. Members from throughout the state participated in the expanded bean industry that included limas; black-eyed peas; and small white and pink, kidney and pinto beans. The general manager for the Oxnard headquarters was A.L. Maddux, while Floyd Broadhead was in charge of field operations in Southern California and Robert Maulhardt Jr. was field representative for Central and Northern California out of Woodland.

A casualty of these down times was the El Rio Warehouse off Vineyard. At one time, the warehouse processed 150,000 sacks of beans a season. By 1969, the production was down to 10,000 sacks. The old milling station would give way to the fifteen-story financial tower building occupied by the Commercial and Farmers National Bank under the guidance of Martin V. Smith and Associates, which became Oxnard's first high-rise.

Oxnard Frozen Foods 1977. *Left to right*: Raymond Swift, John Dullam, Arthur Pidduck, Tom Vujovich, Donald Dufau, David Petit, Joe Terry and John Laubacher (*sitting*). *Andy Hooper.*

By 1970, dry limas accounted for $1.9 million and 7,700 acres in Ventura County. Green limas, grown on 10,100 acres, brought in $3.5 million, and seed limas were grown on 1,200 acres.

By this time, 1970, a new agricultural association had formed, the California Green Lima Bean Growers. The leadership included John T. Dullam from Oxnard as chairman and Bill Connelly (Somis) and Frank McGrath (Camarillo) as board members. Other officers included Lawrence Porter (King City) as vice chairman and Jack Gill (Greenville) as secretary. The association was formed to foster information, promotion and research of green lima beans. One of the major goals of the association was to provide uniform seed quality. Another goal was to promote a program that would emphasize ways to stimulate the consumption of frozen green beans.

Another group formed under the name of the Committee for Improvement of the California Dry Bean Industry. The group was headquartered in Dinuba and included Ventura County representatives Jack Broome, Richard Maulhardt and William McGrath. Their goal was to establish a research and marketing program aimed at improving the returns to growers and handlers through improving bean quality, cookability and digestibility.

The following year, 1971, saw the introduction of two new lima bean varieties: the Westley and the Ventura Bush. The beans were the result of a twenty-year effort by the agronomist from UC Davis. The Westley lima bean was developed to offer a better canning bean. At this point, California was still the number 1 lima bean producer in the nation.

In 1973, longtime bean grower Albert DeBusschere passed away. Albert threshed beans on the Smith Ranch in Camarillo from 1948 to 1960. He also threshed for Rudy Pfeiler on Rice Road as well as for Richard and Jim Naumann of Etting Road.

His son Jesse DeBusschere began threshing for Joe Terry and Bob Friedrich at this time. Jesse started growing and harvesting for himself the following year. He continued farming lima beans for most of the 1970s through 1990, when his son Paul came on board. They partnered until Paul took over the bean operation in 2002.

By 1974, the Pleasant Valley Lima Bean Warehouse was the last remaining of the three remaining warehouses in all of Southern California. The L.A. Hearne Co. out of King City was handling the beans from Central California.

The McGrath family from Montalvo were still growing lima beans at this time. Their lima bean field had the unusual reputation of being the last field in Ventura County to be threshed. This was due to it being located near the coastal area with its damp cool breezes, and it was the last to warm up for planting in the spring and last to dry out in the fall. The property was originally farmed by Hugo McGrath over seventy years before and by this time was farmed by Joe McGrath Jr. Some years, threshing on this ranch wasn't done until January.

A fire in March 1974 at the Kellogg Seed Company warehouse on Front Street in Ventura destroyed the Fordhook lima bean seed stock that the local growers depended on to plant their upcoming crop. While 5,943 acres were planted to green limas in 1974, the acreage almost doubled to 11,000 acres once the seed bank was replenished.

Of the sixty million pounds of lima beans produced in the nation, Ventura County was still producing forty million pounds. The remaining

Art Thomas and sons, Oregon. Thomas farmed the Oxnard Plain for thirty years before moving to Vale, Oregon, in 1987 to farming continue lima beans, taking his thresher. *Left to right*: Jed, Frank, Paul, John, David, Jim and Art (*sitting*). *Thomas family*.

twenty million pounds were produced in King City, Santa Maria, New York and New Jersey.

Many farmers temporarily switched to dry lima beans, and in 1976, they harvested 6,845 acres. Statewide, the average was up 6,000 acres, from 25,000 to 31,000 acres.

One of the few men still threshing in the 1970s and 1980s was Art Thomas. Art sometimes threshed with Bill McLoughlin, and some years he threshed with Bill Maulhardt. In 1977, he added his oldest son, Frank Thomas, to the crew, and they threshed the lima beans for the Nishimori brothers near Pleasant Valley Hospital in Camarillo. Art was on his twenty-sixth year with the same machine, which harvested 2,500 sacks per acre, completing 600 sacks a day. Art would put all of his boys to work in the coming years: Frank, David, Paul, Jimmy, John and Jed. Art recognized the shrinking lima bean acreage meant he had a decision to make, and by 1987, he had relocated his family to Vale, Oregon, where he continued growing beans along with his sons.

Larry Nunes was also still threshing beans at this time. Under the banner of Nunes Custom Farming, Larry farmed the Oxnard Plain for fifty years before passing away in 2000.

Joe Terry was winding down his thirty-seven-year run as a bean thresher. Terry began by purchasing his first thresher from Jim Ward in 1925. The separator was built in 1890 for James Ward and Marion Cannon, who farmed the Mound District. It was later overhauled by blacksmith Cleveland Wiltfong. The machine ended up at the Ventura County Museum but has since been lost to time.

By the end of the '70s, the county was growing green lima beans on 10,600 acres with a value of $7,792,200. Dry limas were produced on 3,115 acres and brought in $2.5 million. The top crop was lemons, which were planted to 23,000 acres and brought in $124 million. Lemons were followed by celery, $53 million; egg production at $43 million; and strawberries at $431 million, grown on only 2,383 acres.

Within a year, in 1980, Ventura County was growing 5,000 acres of dry lima beans and 7,300 acres of limas bound for the freezer. While the acreage of dry limas was reduced by 1985, the Fordhook limas maintained their acreage due to thirty-five growers signed up to sell to Oxnard Frozen Foods. However, the combined acreage of the two dropped to 5,295 acres in 1986 from the almost 10,000 combined acres the previous year.

The decade ended with the lowest production yet of combined green limas, dry limas and green snap beans grown on 2,942 acres. The biggest reason for

Union Ice Company broke ground in Oxnard in 1924 on a forty-five-ton ice plant with three packing sheds. They later partnered Stokely Van Camp to freeze their produce. The company was sold to Terminal Freezers Inc., led by Lowell Dayton, in 1992. *Tim Dayton.*

the decline was the imminent closing of Oxnard Frozen Foods Cooperative. Alpac Food, out of Santa Maria, purchased the co-op's equipment in 1988, and the 38 contracted farmers began making plans for the change. Down to only 160 seasonal workers, only a few years earlier, the company boasted over 1,000 employees.

Within a year, Boskovich Farms purchased the thirteen-acre property. A portion of the facility was leased to Terminal Freezers Inc. out of Oregon. The company, led by Lowell Dayton, came to Oxnard by 1992 after establishing a cold storage business in Watsonville and Salem, Oregon. The Oxnard base was the former home of the Union Ice & Storage Company on East Third Street. The company soon built a 100,000-foot warehouse expansion followed by another 70,000-foot building and a 30,000-processing plant. The company primarily offered storage of fruits, vegetables and fish while offering processing for customers without the ability. Locally grown strawberries, broccoli and lima beans were the main produce to pass through the Oxnard plant.

The company later sold to Lineage Logistics Terminal. Lowell's son Tim Dayton took the cold storage experience he learned from his father and teamed up with Arctic Cold to build a 567,281-square-foot state-of-the-art food processing and cold storage facility off Rice Avenue, Oxnard, that opened in 2022.

The top crop to end the '80s was still lemons, grown on 22,285 acres and bringing in $164,444,000, followed by nursery stock that brought in $93 million and celery at $85 million. Rounding out the top ten were strawberries, Valencia oranges, avocados, lettuce, cut flowers, cabbage and spinach. Lumping dry limas, green limas and green snap beans, the total acreage harvested was 2,942 acres and brought in under $5 million.

The 1990s saw a drop-off in the planting of dry lima beans, but the green limas used for frozen were still viable. With both Stokely and Oxnard Frozen Foods no longer in business, Shaw Frozen Foods filled the gap. They also owned Birds Eye.

In 1993, Kraft General Foods sold its frozen food line operated by Birds Eye to Dean Foods for $140 million. Dean Foods packed and shipped broccoli, Fordhook lima beans, celery and peppers. Five years later, in 1998, Dean Foods would sell to Agrilink for $400 million, and by 2003, Agrilink had closed its Oxnard facility.

By 1997, the combined beans grown in the count were down to 2,559 acres. Bill Lenox grew his limas near the Camarillo Airport, while Jess and Paul DeBusschere farmed on his family's properties on the Oxnard Plan and toward Hueneme. Phil McGrath, whose family farmed lima beans for over one hundred years, dedicated eighteen rows for limas that he sold at farmer's markets. John Borchard and Larry Nunes grew some beans for a few years before Larry retired. Jim Gill grew beans off Laguna Road.

The century ended with 3,528 acres grow to green and dry limas and included snap green beans. The value came in at $5,734,000. The leading crop ending 1999 was strawberries, which brought in over $200 million, grown on 6,592 acres; followed by lemons at $201 million, grown on 27,000 acres; and nursery stock at $139 million, raised on 2,683 acres and 5 million square feet of greenhouses space. Rounding out the top ten crops of Ventura County were celery, Valencia oranges, avocados, cut flowers, tomatoes, broccoli and lettuce.

Bill Lenox continued farming limas for the next decade. Lenox is a third-generation Oxnard farmer. His grandfather John Lenox arrived from Ohio and came to the Oxnard area in 1902. He soon purchased a 120-acre farm off Sturgis Road. He grew sugar beets and lima beans and began leasing an additional 300 acres to grow beans. His son V.G. Lenox purchased an additional ranch of 130 acres. Bill continued the family tradition of farming his family property as well as land near the Camarillo airstrip. Bill farmed until 2014, after which he focused on leasing his farm to berry growers.

Jim Gill also kept the thresher running into the new millennium by growing green limas and later switching to dry limas in 2008. Jim was from a fourth-generation farming family. His great-grandparents Thomas Gill and Katherine Donlon arrived from Ireland in 1883. His grandfather Gregory Gill was running a bean thresher for the Lewis family as early as 1892. Jim planted 600 acres of Fordhooks in 1988. However, other farmers were reducing their output. Tom Vujovich went from planting 1,200 to 700 acres and eventually turned to other crops. Jim continued growing beans for the next twenty years before retiring in 2019. However, his operation was taken on by Mike and Brian Naumann.

From 2001 to 2002, green and dry lima beans dropped in production from 3,162 acres to 1,944. Lemons were the largest harvested crop, though they too saw a drop from 25,864 to 23,603 acres. Strawberries were up to 8,582 acres, but they were bringing in almost $300 million, compared to the beans, which brought in $2,395,000.

By 2008, green, dry lima and snap beans were lumped together with their lowest output for the decade at 1,756 acres. The lone lima bean grower was Paul Debusschere. He would soon be joined by Jim Gill and Mike and Brian Naumann. Their story is told in the "Lima Beans Today" chapter.

4

THE THRESHERS

Threshing machines were a part of the landscape of Ventura County for many years, even before the lima beans were established. The first threshers separated grain seed from the stalks and husks. The machines were hand-fed and horse-powered.

Before the machines, the threshing was done by "tramping" the gathered pods with horses or cattle. The dried vines would be gathered in a circle, and the animals would trod over the vines and pods. Santa Paula–born Arte Duval Donlon provides a description of the process in her book *Memories Are Magic*:

> *The bean vines were tossed to form an immense ring around a flat, open area. A team of horses dragging disks, trod the circle of vines, breaking the pods and causing the beans to fall to the earth. More and more vines were thrown onto the ring until the horses were forced to stop in their circling, the straw was pitched aided and the beans shoved into a center pile. The procedure would be repeated over and over again and the rising pyramid of beans was compensation for the discomfort of dirt and straw-dust that enveloped the workers. They were bandanna masked.*

Some of earliest threshers used a steam engine tractor to pull the machine to the field and then connect to the thresher with a long belt that was powered by a flywheel on the tractor. The parts of a thresher included a threshing cylinder, cylinder casing, concave or concave metal grating surrounded by a cylinder used to rub the grain from the pant, oscillating sieves, a pulley, belts and peg tooth beaters. Later versions included a blower with winnowing or separating capability.

Many times farmers formed partnerships to purchase and use the machine to harvest for other farmers. James Vance and Anton Maulhardt began their partnership as early as 1881. By the next year, Vance had sold his half interest to Maulhardt, and Vance would soon serve as a county supervisor. Maulhardt hired Joe Baxter from the Patterson ranch to run his machine.

Machinists W.H. Dodge put in three months of work to come up with a bean thresher that would not crush the beans. In a November 24, 1883 article, Dodge offered, "I respectfully invite all the bean growers who would encourage the manufacture of a cheap bean thresher in this county, to come out to Judge Wason's place on Monday, November 26th to witness the operation of threshing lima beans reserved for the purpose of testing the merits of the Ventura Bean Thresher."

The 1884 season looked tough for the bean growers because of the abundance of moisture at the beginning, and the fear was the beans would not ripen in time in time for harvesting. Though the prediction did not come true, the gamble of farming was always at play. Alex Gandolfo, who owned a market across the street from the San Buenaventura Mission and who later sold the market to his nephew Nicola Pierano, began advertising to buy the beans in advance in hopes he could capture the market.

In 1885, Jefferson Crane helped transform the cutting of the beans by changing his Minnesota Chief Thresher to cut beans. This revolutionized harvesting beans by limiting the exposure to the rain and winds that can cause major damage to mature beans. "Mr. Crane has the credit of being the first man to thresh lima beans without breaking and damaging the beans."[41]

The next year, he was crowned the "Champion bean thresher of this Valley."[42]

By 1887, there were nine threshing machines in the county that cut either barley or lima beans or both. Ed Ayers started threshing barley on July 6 and finished threshing beans by November 22, 138 days of work, producing 75,520 centals (100 pounds) of barley and 49,416 sacks of beans.

In 1890, James Ward, Marion Cannon and Charles Cook were farmers in the Mound District, the area between Ventura and Montalvo. They hired blacksmith and mechanic Jim Kelly to build a lima bean separator that rose to fifteen feet high, twelve feet wide and forty feet long. Thirty-five years later, in 1925, Joe Terry purchased the thresher from Charles Cook and used it another thirty-seven years near his property near Somis.

13174 THRESHING BEANS, VENTURA CO., CALIF.

Threshing beans in Ventura, California, circa 1910. This image is most likely the Dixie Thompson ranch, which bordered the ocean and was the largest bean field in the world. *Jeff Maulhardt.*

A colorized image of lima beans on the George Hansen Ranch pre-1900 near present-day Sunset Boulevard and Alpine Drive and near Rodeo Drive, Beverly Hills. *Beverly Hills Historical Society and Bison Archives.*

The California Lima Bean Growers Associate created the label brand California Seaside Lima Beans in 1919 for canning labels and for promotion on a national level. *Jeff Maulhardt.*

Frozen foods became popular after World War II. Birds Eye offered frozen green lima beans that became the more familiar lima beans for many who were forced to eat beans in the 1950s and '60s. *Jeff Maulhardt.*

Loren Ayers took this photo in 1848 looking southeast near the Outland Ranch, Santa Paula, with South Mountain in background. *Ayers Family Archives.*

The Daily Brothers thresher later purchased by Dickie Gisler and laid to rest on the Lenox Ranch. *Frank Naumann.*

Nick Sweetland in front of Robert Maulhardt bean thresher, circa 1960s. *Alice Sweetland.*

Frank "Robey" Naumann in a colorized photo from 1952 sitting on a tractor pulling his dad's C.B. Hay thresher. *Frank Naumann.*

A Ventura Manufacturing and Implement, Junior Model No. 2. The thresher was last used in Pomona and rescued by Jim Gill, who donated it to its final home at the Oxnard Historic Farm Park. *Jeff Maulhardt.*

A bean thresher leaving Faria Beach Ranch in 2013, donated by Roberta Baptist, on its way to the Oxnard Historic Farm Park via McCarty and Sons Towing. The machine is thought to have belonged to Frank Beasley of Oxnard in 1914 and later used by Chet Griffith on the Rincon. *Jeff Maulhardt.*

Threshing on the Rincon. The image is labeled John E.B. Merriman, 1953. The Merrimans farmed in Saticoy. Merriman would eventually build an A frame home on Faria Beach, and the thresher ended up on the Faria/Baptiste Ranch. *Roberta Baptiste.*

Art Thomas crew farming Oxnard Plain, 1977. Art is pulling and son Frank is on top. Art Thomas Sr. was one of several important blacksmiths along with Matt and Joe Schreiner and Louis Brenneis, who made implements to improve the farming experience. *Thomas brothers.*

By the 1990s, self-propelled FMC 125 thresher would strip the pods from the cut vines of the green lima beans. These machine could pick up two rows instead of one and they could operate faster than the pulled LV model. *Mike Naumann*.

Larry Nunes of Nunes Custom Farming harvesting large lima beans for Jess and Paul Debusschere on the Lenox Ranch in 1993. Nunez farmed the Oxnard Plain for fifty years. The machine was later purchased by Paul Debusschere in 2004. *Frank Naumann*.

Top: Joey Naumann, sixth-generation farming in action. Planting lima beans in Somis, 2017. *Mike Naumann.*

Bottom: Joey Naumann cultivating lima beans on land he rented from John Orr. *Mike Naumann.*

Top: Bill Lenox crew threshing Camarillo Airbase circa 1993, with the beginning of the Spanish Hills Club golf course back nine in the distance. *Frank Naumann*.

Bottom: Bill Lenox on top of VM&I thresher harvesting between runways at the Camarillo Airport circa 1993. *Frank Naumann*.

Jess and Paul Debusschere threshing the Oxnard Plain, early 1990s. *Frank Naumann.*

Bill Lenox thresher, a Ventura Manufacturing & Implement machine. David Aguilera is the thresherman. Image taken at the foot of the Conejo Grade on the Hiji property. *Bill Lenox.*

Dean Foods cutting Fordhook green lima beans on the Roger's Ranch, owned by the James and Richard Naumann. Round Mountain is in the background, 1999. *Courtesy Mike Naumann.*

The FMC LV was the second-generation viner used by Dean Farms that came out in the late 1960s through the 1980s. These machines could pick up one row at a time. The machine was built as a pea harvester but could be used with the smaller green limas. *Tom Schott.*

Green limas at the Oxnard Frozen Foods plant are transported up a conveyor belt, where the beans will be further cleaned by a shaker and blower before going into a wash tank. *Jeff Maulhardt.*

Left to right, Jess Debusschere with a C.B. Hay; Larry Nunez with a Price thresher; and Tad Deboni, with his Price machine, circa 1990s. *Frank Naumann.*

Joey Naumann atop a 1988 C.B. Hay thresher pulled by a Caterpillar D5B on Jim Gill's Broome Ranch, 2020. *Mike Naumann.*

A 1951 CB Hay machine and 1981 CB Hay thresher. *Mike Naumann.*

Opposite, top: This 1949 International truck originally belonged to Edwin Naumann but was sold to Robert Debusschere (*foreground*). Debusschere's 1948 C.B. Hay thresher is pictured near the Davis ranch off Las Posas Road (*background*). *Frank Naumann.*

Opposite, bottom: The moon rises as the sun sets on Bill Lenox's crew, circa 1993. *Frank Naumann.*

Top: Conner Reiman, a sixth-generation descendant of several early farming families, waving atop a 1958 CB Hay thresher pulled by a Caterpillar D5 off Cawelti Road on the Sakioka Ranch. *Jeff Maulhardt.*

Bottom: Jess DeBusschere driving a Caterpillar D4 7 U series pulling a 1948 C.B. Hay thresher on the Friedrich Ranch on Pleasant Valley Road, 1992. *Frank Naumann.*

Mike Naumann leading the way atop a 1981 C.B. Hay thresher followed by son Joey Naumann atop a 1957 C.B. Hay and the third operated by Mason Parker on a 1988 C.B. Hay, 2023. The threshers are pulled by a combination of Caterpillar D5Bs and D4E. *Jeff Maulhardt.*

Old Oxnard thresher laid to rest near old boney mountain on Pepe Sanchez Ranch. *Jeff Maulhardt.*

Waite Gerry was originally from New York and Pennsylvania. He came to the Ventura County in 1873 and by 1880 had purchased seventy-five acres in the Mound District, east Ventura and Montalvo area. In May 1891, Gerry took a visit to the East Coast. By August, a bean thresher from Fleetwood, Pennsylvania, had arrived. The cost for the freight of car was $300. Gerry was from a mechanical background, and he used his skill to improve his thresher over the years. He invented the double cylinder as well as a cleaning attachment for threshing beans.[43]

The new bean threshers were subject to many experiments and changes. In September 1892, Henry G. Bennison, a blacksmith from Santa Paula, found out "that the wagon-wheel to which that endless chain was attached for communicating power to the machine was too light and would not revolve but slide along the ground; so he sent away for heavy castings and he would rig it so that both rear wheels of the wagon could convey power to the cylinder of the thresher."[44]

Others who were threshing in 1892 included Gregory Gill, who was working on the Lewis bean thresher on the Colonia on the Kaufman ranch in July, where he was joined Daniel Ross, who finished threshing for J.E. Borchard. The Donlon thresher "cleaned out" all the ranches along the riverbank. Over in Springville, Rice & Hartman's bean thresher was at work by September on a tract east of the Baptist church. Louis

Steam engine. The steam engine was first used in the county as early as 1890 and replaced the draft horses used to pull the thresher. *Oxnard Historic Farm Park.*

Maulhardt was threshing Lady Washington beans in September while waiting for his limas to dry. Scott Saviers was also using his bean thresher by September. Joseph Lewis from Montalvo was still threshing beans in October.

In 1893, R.C. Sudden used "The Minnesota Chief" thresher, a premium machine of the day invented in 1875. The Donlon Brothers machine was threshing beans for Archie Connelly and produced over a ton an acre before moving on to the Milligan ranch. Richardson's thresher did work on Feld Grace's lima beans. Louis Maulhardt, son of Jacob, had a new combine bean thresher different from barley machines that did not crack the beans and had a double cylinder, an extra fan and a clod crusher. A.B. "Pap" Smith from Las Posas employed Jake Markle as his chief engineer for his thresher.

In 1894, Borchard and & Petit Brothers, J. Maulhardt, J.C. Hartman and Donlon Bros. threshed eighty thousand sacks of barley by August 10.

Under "Colonia Cullings" from the *Ventura Free Press* on October 18, 1895; "The Maulhardt machine has been threshing for Zach Graham and Hugh Henry. Joseph Lewis threshed for Archie Connelly from 35 acres of lima beans 1,250 sacks, averaging 2,700 pounds per acre. Donlon brothers beans on the Hollister tract. Petit Brothers, Maulhardt & Saviers threshing outfits were at work in September, 1895."

In August 1896, Louis Maulhardt hired the Union Oil Company in Santa Paula to build a "monster" boiler to be used in the threshing machine he was having built. It was the largest boiler of the kind in the county at thirty horsepower and weighing eight tons.

D.S. Cook also had a new machine built that he built in own shop. He also added a train of ten new wagons from Sheldon & Vickers. "This is the sort of enterprise that circulates coin among people."[45]

Gill brothers Greg, Thomas and James threshed beans from Santa Susana to Somis to Camarillo and back to the Oxnard Plain. Their parents, Thomas Gill and Catherine Donlon Gill, arrived from County Longford, Ireland, in 1886. *Museum of Ventura County, photograph 25457 OS.*

Many of the farmers for the different districts formed c-operatives to purchase a bean thresher that they then shared. Many of the bean growers on the Oxnard Plain formed partnerships with another farmer or they owned their individual machine. Then they'd service the lima beans on the north side of the river. However, many of these farmers grew impatient with the timeline and took things into their own hands.

As early as 1901, the Mound Threshing Company was formed to harvest lima beans in the district. The participants bought an old separator and did their own work. Among the farmers who formed the group were Messrs. Dunning, McKenzie, Price, Harkey, Walters, Gerry, Smith, Hall and Isham. Meetings took place at the home of Will Dunning. They purchased a mammoth traction engine from the Avery Company of Peoria, Illinois. G.E. Gerry was in charge of the machine, and Mr. Isham would secure the work. Vincent Savory acted as the roustabout, loading and unloading and other needed duties. They would take on jobs from Las Posas to as far away as Fillmore and Bardsdale.

Other districts followed. The Saticoy Threshing Company purchased a machine built by J.H. Kelley. The Moorpark Threshing Company purchased an engine from the Russell Manufacturing Company. For the Foothill Threshing Company, Ed Barlow served as the separator boss, and Carl Fowler ran the engine. The Ventura-Camarillo Threshing Company purchased a thirty-six-by-sixty-cylinder machine from Ventura Implement and Manufacturing Company. The directors of this group included Adolfo Camarillo, J.D. McGrath, J.B. Jewett, J.H. Drake and C.L. Chrisman.

Among the other threshing outfits during this time were Edwards & Petit, Ward and Cannon, Frank Cook, Joseph Lewis, Gill Brothers (Gregory, Thomas and James), M.V. Carr, Donlon Brothers, George Cook, Diedrich Brothers, O.B. Dunn & Clarence Chrisman, Naumann Brothers, Louis G. Maulhardt, Thermal Belt Threshing Company, R.C. Sudden, O.A. Wadleigh, Frank Petit, Patterson Ranch Company, J.B. Dawley, George C. Power and Hill Brothers.

The mechanic who worked on many of these machines was James F. Fulkerson, from Oxnard Implement and Carriage Works, located at the corner of A and Fourth Streets. Fulkerson set up shop with the formation of the town of Oxnard in 1898. He brought in a big steam hammer that weighed eleven tons. He was soon renovating and adjusting threshing machines to meet the needs of the farmer. His first project was for Louis Maulhardt, followed by a complete construction for E.R. and R.N. Hill that included a separator, derrick, table, net beds and cookhouse. Fulkerson also ran the machines for his clients.

His brother, Jonathon Fulkerson, was also in the business of working on the machines. He founded a blacksmith shop in Somis in 1891 and expanded to a hardware store in 1912 that the family still operates under the guidance of his grandson Bob Fulkerson.

In March 1903, several of the Ventura machine shops bound together to form the Ventura Manufacturing and Implement Company. The goal was to manufacture, repair, buy and sell threshing machines, wagons, carriages, engines, motors, belts, chains, tools and attachments of all kinds of machinery; to manufacture, buy and sell agricultural implements, paints, oils, distillates, etc.; and to do general foundry work. The seven directors were William F. Hamilton, George C. Power, J.H. Chaffee, J.S. Collins, W.H. Barnes, William McGuire and R.C. Sudden. The capital stock was $25,000 divided into five hundred shares and $50 a share.

Hamilton came up with the majority of the early inventions and patents. Among his many inventions were the bean planter, clod crushers, bean

James F. Fulkerson's lima bean threshing outfit. James made several threshers for local farmers from his blacksmith shop, the Oxnard Implement and Carriage Works. His brother Jonathon opened a blacksmith shop in Somis in 1891. *Museum of Ventura County, photograph 2332 OS.*

cultivators, beet drills, an adjustable belt guide and several types of chisels. Within the next several decades, the VM&I company shipped equipment to South Africa, Somalia and Europe.

The company also collaborated with the local farmers. Scott Saviers was the son of James Young Saviers. J.Y. Saviers was born in Ohio in 1824. He took the journey across the Great Plains in 1850 and began mining near Hangtown, California. He was a wagon maker by trade and opened up a shop in Shingle Springs, Amador County. While out hunting, he was shot by Indians in both shoulders as well as in the head. He returned to Ohio in 1860 with his wife, Elizabeth Joes. He later settled in Yuba County until 1863, when he moved to Sutter County. In October 1869, Saviers moved once again to what is present-day Oxnard in Santa Barbara County and purchased acreage from Thomas Bard. Saviers later served as the justice of the peace for Hueneme Township.

Winfred Scott Saviers was born in 1861, and by the early 1890s, he was making adjustments to his threshing machine to cut beans more efficiently. He invented a separator that could thresh lima beans, barley, wheat and oats. He also built a bean planter he was selling by 1902. Once Ventura Manufacturing and Implement Company began operations, Saviers split his discoveries with the company.

The company was offering a slightly smaller, Ventura Junior bean thresher by 1915. By 1918, the company had announced that it would be offering a pickup-type bean thresher. It also announced the building of a new factory site in Ventura that would have twenty thousand square feet of manufacturing space located at 1056 East Front Street.

In 1933, the VM&I built a new steel pickup bean thrasher. This new machine required the work of six men to harvest compared to the forty men needed to service a stationary machine. To demonstrate the new machine, the public was invited to the Maulhardt Ranch off Rose Road (now Avenue) to view the machine purchased by Robert and John Maulhardt.

The company went through many changes over the years. In July 1840, eighty-year-old George C. Power, an original trustee, took on sole ownership and placed Milan J. Wright as his general manager. In May 1943, George Power passed away and the company was in the hands of Hermann Wechsler and B.E. Kulper Sr. However, they dissolved the partnership by 1948. A few years later, in 1950, the building was partially burned.

The company was revived in Oxnard and by 1974 was owned by Alvin Aggen. The new location was at 1265 Commercial Avenue, and the company was taking on other manufacturing duties.

In 1906, the Saticoy Threshing Co. began its operations in the area. The machine was owned by Saticoy farmers Brown, A. Endergat, Smith and Culp. One of their first jobs was threshing the beans for Marple-Farwell and Robert L. Owens.

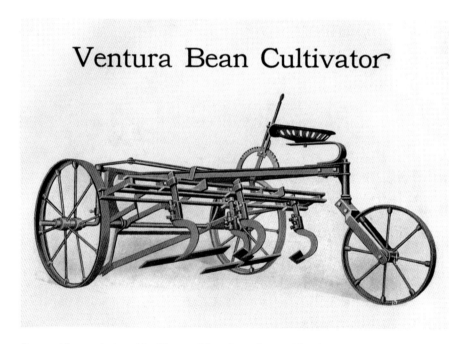

Bean cultivator designed by Ventura Manufacturing and Implements. Many times, local farmers brought their ideas to the company to produce a more efficient implement. *Craig Held.*

The Robert and John Maulhardt thresher built by Ventura Manufacturing and Implement Company. A demonstration was held at the Maulhardt home ranch in 1933. *Jeff Maulhardt.*

Remie Callens arrived in Ventura County in 1881 from Belgium. He purchased land in the Ocean View District off Hueneme Road. He owned a bean thresher from Ventura Manufacturing and Implement in conjunction with James Leonard. By 1918, he was working with Cleve Wiltfong to build his own thresher machines out of his barn and sell them to the local farmers. Callens installed an electric lighting plant on his bean thresher. By using his lights, he did not need to burn any straw, and the lighting system made it so that the sacking tent was better lighted than the day. However, after struggling to obtain enough labor, Callens sold his machine to Albert Wucherpfennig.

A game changer was introduced in 1918 by the Harris Manufacturing Company out of Stockton. Its new thresher was able to go through the fields, picking up the beans cleaner than ever done by hand. It carried the sacked beans and dropped the sacks in piles. It operated with five men instead of forty to forty-five. The machine had a capacity of sixty to ninety sacks a day and covered thirty acres a day. The new thresher cost $5,500. The new machine went to work on Ventura County farms, including the C.L. Chrisman ranch in Santa Paula and in Camarillo for the Daily brothers, Andrew Cawelti, Wilber Styles and J.T. O'Connor.

C.B. Hay was a machinist from San Jose who helped modernize the lima bean thresher. He was born Colin Brody Hay in Tracy, San Joaquin

County, California, on January 6, 1887. By 1910, he was working as a machinist in San Jose. In 1923, he was rebuilding bean threshers for A.H. Averhill Machinery Co., distributors of the Russell Bean Threshers. He rebuilt a thirty-seven-by-forty-six Russell Bean thresher with a feeder and a blower and advertised in the *Sacramento Bee* in 1923. Two years later, he was advertising the sale of the "Go Getter" Pick Up Bean Harvester for $2,250. Soon after, the C.B. Hay Company began manufacturing threshers on request. The Depression years of 1927 and through most of the 1930s was slow business for most workers at the time, including Hay, but 1929 saw a new C.B. Hay machine delivered to W.A. Kennedy in Salinas.

By 1938, Hay had teamed up with the engineers at the College of Agriculture at Davis, who spent three years experimenting on improvements to the thresher. The big innovation was the use of rubber rollers instead of the spiked cylinders used on other threshers. The idea was based on the concept used in a washing machine wringer whereby the beans would experience less damage to the seed, and this led to a higher germination percentage. The machine was equipped with six rubber rollers in three pairs. The rollers were thirty-six inches long, twelve inches in diameter and coated with a half inch of pure rubber. The upper sets of rollers revolved faster than the lower sets, giving a rubbing effect that readily separated the beans from the pods. Lumps of dirt were pulverized by the rollers and the dust ejected by blowers. The result was a cleaner product.[46]

The machine was initially used to harvest red kidney beans, but by the following year, the developers focused on adjusting the machine to harvest lima beans. Frank Borchard was the first to test the new thresher in the fall of 1939. One of biggest differences in the C.B. Hay threshers was the smaller size compared to other machines.

Within a few years, they built a "Big Bertha" version that was forty-nine and a half inches wide. The machine was designed by Roy Bainer and J. Stanley Winters and manufactured by C.B. Hay, who retained the rights

Callens and Leonard bean threshing outfit. Remy Callens built many of the early threshers. Many of these same workers came from the Azores. *Joe Donlon.*

to the manufacturing. Albert Pfeiler and his son-in-law Albert DeBusschere purchased a three-cylinder, fifty-foot machine in 1948. The receipt shows the machine was "Set up for bulk, to be converted in '49." The thresher was ordered with a bulk bin that wasn't ready, so a sack house was accepted and then replaced with the bulk bin. The sack house was removed the following year and used as a bunkhouse.

John Broome also bought a Big Bertha C.B. Hay machine in 1949. Broom's machine included a six-volt lighting system and a Hercules JXD engine.

With the demand for frozen food after the end of World War II, many farmers turned to planting the Fordhook lima bean, suited for quick freeze packaging. A new way of threshing these beans was developed with the introduction of "Viner" machines. In 1947, Ventura Farms Frozen Foods, led by Tom Leonard, began building a vining plant off Vineyard Avenue near El Rio.

While similar to the dry farming process, the timing and equipment for harvesting was much different. From the time the bean plant is cut in the field until the beans are frozen and stored for shipment, only a matter of a few hours elapse. Cutting, windrowing and loading in the field was done in the same method as dry beans, except the beans are hauled to the plant for processing as soon as they are cut instead of left on the field to dry. The plant installed eight Viners. However, portable Viners were also used in the fields. After being cut, the beans move up a conveyor belt while the beans are constantly shaken and separated from the pod. The beans were loaded into containers and immediately iced before being shipped to a processing plant.

Yet there was still a demand for dry limas, and improvements to threshers followed. In October 1953, Urban Underwood of Moorpark introduced

Top: Bob Pfeiler spent several years photographing local agriculture. This picture from the 1940s shows John F. Petit threshing beans on his Price thresher. *Robert Pfeiler.*

Bottom: Robert Naumann in front of his CB hay thresher, circa 1950. *Frank Naumann.*

Opposite: By 1948, a new combine had been introduced. These images show the cutting, loading and icing of green lima beans before they are trucked to the packinghouse. *Mike Naumann.*

a new type of thresher pulling unit, a two-wheeled, rubber-tired tractor using a hydro-motor steering system powered by a V-8 passenger car engine. The pulling made it possible with its two transmissions to move the thresher easily through the fields and also move speedily along the highways between jobs.[47]

Underwood's grandson Craig Underwood continued the tradition of threshing beans into the 1970s. "I can remember as a kid liking pulling the net back into the wagons after unloading the vines and beans from the wagons into a stationary machine. Then dad (Richard) and Neil operated three mobile machines, one self propelled (a Price Thresher)."[48]

Craig Underwood has fond memories despite harvesting beans from 7:00 a.m. to 7:00 p.m. several weeks at a time. Fighting the Santa Ana winds was always a challenge. One week during heavy winds, Craig recalled starting at 7:00 a.m. and threshing until midnight.

Craig says he has lima beans in his blood. That makes sense, since he was born during the height of bean harvesting, October 4. In fact, his dad was on his machine when Craig's mom went into labor. He would later trade his lima bean seeds in for red jalapeño peppers to make his popular Sriracha Dragon Sauce.

By 1965, Oxnard Frozen Foods had purchased nine mobile combines manufactured by FMC Corporation out of San Jose, the FMC LV. These first combines were pulled by a tractor. After the vines were cut at the ground level and windrowed, the combine followed, scooping up the vines and empty pods and depositing them back on the ground for nitrogen value. The green beans would go into a large hopper on the combine and were loaded into waiting trucks for transporting to the plant, where they were washed, graded, packaged and frozen, all within one and a half hours after

Fordhook green limas being dumped into truck. Green limas became popular after World War II and the demand for frozen foods rose. Once cut, harvested and loaded into awaiting trucks, the process took less than two hours compared to weeks with older methods. *Mike Naumann.*

being harvested. By the next year, Oxnard Frozen Foods was up to twenty-five combine machines.

By the 1980s, Oxnard Frozen Foods was using self-propelled pea harvesters, known as "tank trucks," FMC H-2. The last model used in the area was the FMC 125. Dean Foods also used the FMC 125 in the 1990s. Tom Schott worked for Dean Foods and explained that these machines were actually built for harvesting peas but were also used for the green lima beans. While the machine was used to strip the peas from the pods, Tom pointed out that it worked better to cut the lima beans windrow before the plant was fed through the head at the front of the machine.

While the majority of Viner machines have left the Oxnard Plain, there are still several C.B. Hay and other pickup threshers harvesting dry lima beans in the fall on the Oxnard Plain along the roads of Las Posas, Cawelti and Laguna and on over to Hueneme Road.

5

THE WORKERS

Planting lima beans did not take a large crew. Likewise, maintaining the crop did not take many workers to keep the fields free of weeds. However, in the early days before the pickup threshers and self-propelled machines, a large crew of transitory workers was necessary.

The first method of harvesting was the "tramping out" of beans. A large plot was leveled, and the dried bean vines were placed in a circle as horse teams and carts, disks or wagons were driven over the plants until well broken. The straw was sifted out with large pitchforks and the beans on the ground sacked.

Harvesting the beans with a thresher machine required a large crew of thirty to fifty men. The bean threshing season could last between thirty and sixty days depending on the weather and the condition of the beans. Each ranch might take up to a week or more to thresh depending on the size of the acreage.

The early workers consisted of the older sons of the farmer plus crews of transient seasonal workers. The Chinese population near the San Buenaventura Mission became a labor source for the early harvesting years.

In 1887, Sam Fong Yi set up an employment office and general merchandise store in China Alley near the San Buenaventura Mission. The ad in the paper promised "satisfaction guaranteed" for his workers.

Another person who was instrumental in supplying labor for the farmers was Tom Lim Yan. Tom came to Ventura County in the 1870s. He started a school in 1878. It was noted in the paper that "Tom Lim Yan was one of

Munger Brothers bean threshing, Santa Paula. The tool wagon is on left with knapsacks on top, with the "Doghouse" or sewing tent on the right. *Pleasant Valley Historical Society, courtesy Bill Milligan.*

the most intelligent and highly educated Chinamen we have ever met. He speaks and writes English fluently and looks after the school, of which he seems very proud."

He owned a store called Kun Wo and Company located on Figueroa Street in San Buenaventura. In an 1894 article, the *Ventura Free Press* pointed out that a good many people were getting their lima beans picked by "Chinamen." Louis Pfeiler from the Colonia Rancho had 1,600 sacks repacked, of which 57 sacks were bad ones. Labor cost ninety-six dollars.[49]

From a December 27, 1895 article in the *Ventura Free Press*, we learn that the workers earned a different amount per hour depending of the skill of the job. The man running the separator operator was paid the most at $6.00 a day. Next in line was the engineer at $4.00. The sack sewers and sack tender were paid $3.00 a day. The three feeders and the fireman got $2.00 an hour, and the three hoe downs were paid $1.75 a day while the oiler, straw buck, derrick tender and pitcher all received $1.50 a day. Wagon drivers, between five and ten men, were paid $1.25 a day. The water buck earned $30 a month, and the cook and his helper received $60 a month.

Joe Terry came to Ventura County in 1906 with his parents from the Azores. He gave an interview to the *Ventura County Star* published on June 27, 1975. The interview was later a part of *Ventura County Historical Quarterly*. Terry said in the early threshing days, it took fifty-two men, thirty-eight horses, fourteen wagons and a steam engine needed to keep the lima bean separator running without a letup.

Terry began working with his father as a boy in the 1910s. Terry Sr. used hire Pala Indians for his harvesting crew. They were from the San Luis River valley in northern Sand Diego County. Terry remembered one hardworking Indian named Richard Attache who actually played football at Carlisle with Olympic champion Jim Thorpe. After working all week, Terry would drop off his crew in downtown Oxnard and turn them loose. During the early 1920s, Oxnard had an active nightlife with multiple saloons and an underground that including gambling and other illegal offerings.

Terry also pointed out that he could rely on a workforce that followed the harvest. "Men who followed the harvests would show up for the bean harvest and in 30 to 40 days the crop would be sacked. Then they'd leave for some other crop harvest. It was no trouble at all to round up a crew. We'd just drive out to where they lived, sometimes in a lean-to under the gum trees and recruit a crew in short order."

There was a barranca area in Somis where temporary workers gathered. Many came during the Dust Bowl years in the 1930s. The area was called "hobo jungle."

Arthur Mahan was a farmer, and he too relied on the workers from the hobo jungle. He pointed out that they were called "bundle stiffs" because many of them used to carry a bundle of clothes or bedding on their backs. Mahan recalled hiring up to sixty workers because you never knew when one would leave. They were paid between $2.50 and $3.00 a

Twenty-nine-man crew on lima bean sacks, circa 1900. *Craig Held.*

day, and he'd collect the workers a few days in advance so many of them could sober up and be fed and ready to work long hours. One of his returning workers was called "Nuts and Bolts" because he didn't know the difference between a nut and bolt or much of anything else. Yet he was adept at driving a bean wagon.

The Portuguese workforce was instrumental in the growth of the lima bean industry. Among the first to arrive in Ventura County in 1873 were Manuel Jacinto and Antone Silva. A few years later, in 1877, came Fales Oliver, William Oliver and Joe Enos. John Manuel came in 1878. Antone Baptiste was only fourteen when he arrived in 1883. By 1900, with the establishment of the sugar beet factory and the strong growth of the lima bean industry, more men from the Azores found employment in Ventura County.

Manuel Faria arrived in 1903 and found work on the Patterson Ranch. While riding his horse along the coastline past Ventura, Faria later remarked to his daughter Virginia that he felt like he'd returned to his homeland of Fayal and was looking at the islands of St. George and Pico. By 1914, he owned 325 acres of beachfront farmland.

Many of the Portuguese would band tighter to work for several of the local farmers. Both James Leonard and Louis Maulhardt hired a Portuguese crew that included Will Rogers, Otto Moreno, John Domingos, Frances Durate and Frank Dutra, supplemented with Ventura-born Andrew Lorenzana.

Another popular gathering spot for seasonal workers starting in September was at the corner of Fifth Street and Saviers (Oxnard Boulevard today) in Oxnard. One of the larger crews in 1915 was for the Callens and Leonard outfit, which needed sixty-five men to take on the Henry Maulhardt Ranch. C.J. Keller became the field boss for this job.

Others gathering men at this time included Tom Gill, who was headed to Moorpark. The Donlon machine went to Las Posas, and the Petit and McLoughlin machines stayed local.

Other threshers in the field were at the Ward Machine at the Pat Flynn homeplace near Camarillo; Paul Penland in upper Las Posas; John Petit on the Gabe Gisler ranch, Springville; Frank Petit on the Charles Daily ranch; Louis Maulhardt on his Santa Rosa Valley ranch; Tom Steele on the Rostler ranch; Gill Bros. on the Morris Cohn Ranch, Frank Wadleigh and Dam Emmett, upper Las Posas; Callens and Leonard, Callens ranch; Patterson Ranch Co. in Simi; and Cook and Valentine working Saticoy.

The cookhouse was a staple of the lima bean harvest. Longtime Ventura County farmer Bill Milligan explained to Joy Todd, a docent from the Pleasant Valley Historical Society, that the cook was the most important asset to a threshing outfit and that many of the workers would seek out the best cooks in choosing who to work for.

A young Katherine McLoughlin Godfrey, daughter of Oxnard farmer Thomas McLoughlin, remembered eating at the cookhouse. "We had cook houses on the field for the purpose of feeding the laborers, but we kids would eat with them. I vividly recall Mr. Gee, our Chinese cook,

Top: Montalvo workers at the Montalvo Warehouse. Workers come to Ventura County during harvest season, which could start as early as September and end in November. *Eric Daily.*

Bottom: Diedrich Brothers, Louis and John, off Rose Avenue, Oxnard. The cookhouse in the back served not only the workers during the threshing time but also the families. *Pleasant Valley Historical Society.*

because he made pies that would melt in your mouth. On either side of the cook house were long benches on which we all ate and we ate Mr. Gee's delectable food."[50]

Katherine wrote that she and her siblings earned extra money by picking through the threshed beans. "After school and Saturdays we would go out and pick the settings, because the threshers would not pick up all the beans. We made our own square boxes with screens on the bottom. After putting in the bean straw we would sift the boxes and then tale the beans and put them in a sack. Our mother would pay us for the beans we had picked."

In August 1918, the Ventura County Lima Bean Threshers Association met to determine wages for the upcoming harvest. Edmund Garry was elected as chairman, and Joseph McGrath was selected as secretary. The agreed-on wages were as follows: sack sewers, $4.50; hoedowners, $4.50; feeders, $5.00; pitchers, $3.00; drivers, $2.25; strawbucks, three men, $3.00 each; derrick drivers, $3.00; oilers, $4.00; firemen, $3.50; water buck, $3.00; cook and helper, $10.00.

Sack sewers developed a skill that relied on speed and accuracy and were much sought after. Frank Miranda had a long career as a sack sewer. He

The Enoch Waters crew of twenty-nine workers. Waters was from Tennessee and arrived in 1911. He farmed in both Oxnard and Camarillo. Having a good cook ensured the best crew. *Chuck Covarrubias.*

Farel Ayers transporting one-hundred-pound sacks of lima beans near Briggs and Telegraph Road, Santa Paula, circa 1905. Ayers arrived from Missouri in 1888 when he was ten years old. *Ayers Family Archives.*

worked for many of the early threshing outfits, from Henry Beasley in 1914 to Chet Griffith in 1953.

However, many of these jobs were eliminated with the introduction of the next-generation threshers that included the pickup portion of the machine and simplified harvest work.

In some cases, the cookhouse was used beyond harvesting time. Joe Lewis Jr. and his wife hosted a group of friends for a "novel luncheon" in October 1926 at his cookhouse near Camarillo. Using the usual cooks for the crew, Lewis served lunch to Mr. and Mrs. Loren Working, Mr. and Mrs. Noble Powell and Mr. and Mrs. Edwin Carty.

The war years were also a challenge during harvest time. In October 1918, the city trustees of Oxnard met with the ranchers, the owners of the threshers and the saloon owners. The complaint was that there were not enough men to harvest the beans and beets, and part of the problem was that the available men were getting drunk in saloons and missing work. The trustees agreed to close the saloons for two weeks as a way to aid the war effort so the crews could stay together to harvest the crops for the troops. City attorney Charles Blackstock supported the trustees' position.

Among the bean thresher owners who signed the petition were B.F. Barr, Borchard & Petit Bros., Bert Culbert, Donlon Brothers, J.B. Dawley, D.W. Emmett, Tom Gill, Gisler Brothers, Wm. M. Haydock, J.W. Hitch,

Top: The long workday required a shaded tent and some bedding as crews worked around the clock. *Oxnard Historic Farm Park.*

Bottom: Workers for lima bean season could be found near the barranca in Somis as well as Fifth Street in Oxnard. *Eric Daily.*

Joe F. Lewis, Louis G. Maulhardt, D. McGrath Estate Co., Munger Bros., Paul Naumann, John F. Petit, Fred Pidduck, B. Schmitz and Frank O. Wadleigh.

During the Depression years of the 1930s, the bean thresher workers were paid accordingly: loaders, $2.50 a day; drivers $2.00; feeders $4.00; hoe-downs $4.00; fillers $4.50; sawbucks $4.00; derrick drivers $2.75; net hookers $2.00; and oilers $4.00. The year-round jobs included separator man, engine man, water buck, caterpillar and roustabout.[51]

Sack sewers were paid a little more. Jose "Chief" Ortega and Urban Underwood gained a reputation for their skill. Ortega explained the process to the local paper: "Under an awning at the side of the rig the beans poured out into a two sided outlet. When one sack was filled as the flow of the beans were diverted to into another. A sack sewer had to whip a row of stitches into the top of the sack and be ready when the next flow of beans came his way."[52] The one-hundred-pound bags were then tossed into a row of sacked beans that could reach up to several feet high.

The pickup threshers were introduced in the early 1920s and slowly became the standard for most outfits by the 1940s. A work crew dropped from fifty men to a minimum of six. No longer were the beans delivered to the stationary machine. With the pickup version, the equipment picks up the beans on the left of the thresher. A revolving belt arrangement fitted over a shovel-nosed attachment slid easily and smoothly along under the windrow and the beans moved easily up into a carrier and into the thresher.

The viners used in harvesting green limas in the late 1940s quickly evolved to eventually being self-propelled all-in-one machines (more info in the Thresher chapter).

One job that stuck around and has always been a part of any agricultural endeavor is the field walker, a person who walked the fields for a grower or maybe a fertilizer distributor or seed distributor. Oxnard Frozen Foods had several young men connected to the farming families of the area who performed this duty. Among the field walkers in the 1980s were Mike Friel, Andy Hooper, Ned Laubacher, Jack McGrath, Pete Nyarady and Chris Oliva. In addition to reporting the condition of the Fordhook crop to the company, the walkers would eliminate any rogue plants that might affect the production of the beans. A little later, Gerry Benson, who went on to become a master gardener of Ventura County, walked for Duda Farms.

Workers in the warehouses were predominately female. Adele Flynn Walsh remembers her grandmother Clara Williams Hernandez working at

The ladies of Pleasant Valley packinghouse circa the 1930s. Identified here are Winifred Allen Chunn (*back row, far right*) and Clara Williams Hernandez (*front row, far right*). *Mary Caroline Chunn.*

the plant in Camarillo, and during the Depression, the ladies would take turns working so they all had a chance to work.

Rosie Razo grew up on Enterprise Street in Oxnard, and when Stokely–Van Camp opened in the 1946, she and her lady friends all jumped at a chance to work together at the plant. Many of these ladies worked at the facility for thirty years. Among the ladies who joined Rosie at Stokely were Jean Almeida, Margaret Castro, Frances Castro Chacon, Louise Garcia, Mary Gonzales, Ethel Sims, Rachel Pedraza, Helen Rodriguez and Martha Vera.

All these factory jobs would give way to mechanization and automation.

Not all workers in the fields were young men. Tad DeBoni was ninety-one and still working in the bean harvest in 2003, completing his seventy-second year in the fields. He began harvesting in 1931, and seventy years later he was working for Paul Debusschere and sharing his decades of bean knowledge. DeBoni was in charge of fixing chains, repairing parts and overseeing the operation.

Today, Paul DeBusschere plants the seed by himself. Mike and Brian Naumann do their own planting, and James Reiman relies on the workers at Rio Farms to plant the seed he harvests. Cutting the beans can also be a one-man job, but harvesting may take a few extra men to cover the potential problems.

Paul DeBusschere points out that ideally an operation would have a driver and an operator for each machine and another driver to unload and a mechanic/fabricator on standby in case the seventy-five-year-old thresher breaks down.

And then there's the weather. As long as the Santa Ana winds don't mutilate the vines and the rain doesn't interrupt the harvesting, the lima beans will make it to the market.

6

LIMA BEANS TODAY

Like many crops and many communities, the lima bean was replaced with other successful crops and the land was replaced with asphalt, houses and progress. Ventura County isn't the only place that thrived on producing beans. In 1918, James Irvine from Orange County grew limas on thirty-seven square miles of farmland. While this translated into a lot of income, growing houses and malls produced even more money. Fortunately for Ventura County, a few longtime farming families have continued to grow lima beans into the twenty-first century.

Today, California is the only state in the United States to grow the dry large lima beans. These beans need a long growing season and are sensitive to high humidity. California's coastal climate offers warm days and cool nights with morning fog in the spring months that create the perfect climate for superior beans.

Lima beans are still grown in the coastal valleys of California, from Morgan Hill in the north to Camarillo in the south, a span of 330 miles.

As recently as 2014, California was the seventh-largest bean producer in the United States, which translates to 5 percent of the nation's bean crop. North Dakota, Michigan and Delaware are also producers of lima beans, but California is the only state to produce the dry lima bean crop.

The 2023 season was a tough year for bean growers in California. With record rains in the spring, most crops were not planted until May and June. Then, just as the beans were about to begin drying out, Ventura County experienced a once-in-a-lifetime event on August 20, a torrential rain that was associated with Hurricane Hilary that was categorized as the wettest tropical cyclone in state history. The heavy downpour dropped nearly three inches of rain over several hours. To top it off, once the beans were ready to be harvested, the Santa Ana winds wreaked havoc on the cut beans. Mike and Brian Naumann faced windswept rows measuring almost six feet high, making it impossible to untangle the vines. The Naumanns were forced to burn a portion of their unsalvageable beans.

Given all that, California farmers still produced 13,300,000 pounds of dry limas, off about 25 percent. Fortunately, the 2024 crop looks promising, as long as Mother Nature doesn't interfere.

The market for the beans includes the southern states, along the Eastern Seaboard and in the United Kingdom and Italy. Approximately one thousand tons of dry limas are shipped in two-ton (four thousand) tall totes to the United Kingdom and Italy from the Hearne Company warehouse in King City. The best of these dry lima beans come from Ventura County.

With the closing of the Oxnard Frozen Foods facility in 1988 and later the sale of Deans Foods in 1998 and finally the closing of Agrilink Frozen Foods

Lee lima bean seeds are delivered to Mike Naumann by LA Hearne Company. Hearne will also pick up the beans, clean the beans and distribute them. *Mike Naumann.*

Jesse and son Paul Debusschere next to their 1957 D4 Caterpillar tractor that pulled an 1848 standard CB Hay on the Friedrich Ranch of Pleasant Valley Road, south of Camarillo Airport, 1992. *Frank Naumann.*

in 2003, the green lima bean production has fallen into a sharp decline. However, the county still grows the Fordhook lima beans used for frozen foods. Pictsweet Farms, a company that has been around for seventy-five years, still plants and harvests green lima beans.

The production of lima beans in Ventura County almost came to a stop but was saved by a fifth-generation county farmer. Paul DeBusschere is the link between the past and present. Paul has been planting and harvesting lima beans since 1992, when he joined his father, Jesse Debusschere. For a few years, he was the "Lone Ranger" growing limas.

Paul is a fifth-generation lima bean grower dating back to 1890, when Louis Pfeiler, Paul's great-great-grandfather, planted fifty acres of lima beans. Paul's great-grandfather Rudy Pfeiler also farmed limas near Fifth Street and Rice Road. Paul's great-grandfather on his father's side, Hector DeBusschere, arrived from Bissegem, Belgium, in 1909. He traveled with the Remie Callen's family, who were also from Belgium and were returning from a trip to their old home. Both farmed off Hueneme Road. Hector worked for several local farmers, whom he claimed aided his learning of farming. He worked on the Callens Ranch, Justin Petit Ranch, Judge Daly

Ranch in Ojai and the Frank Gisler Ranch off Hueneme Road. By 1916, he was able to purchase the property. Hector's son Albert Debusschere took over farming limas in the 1930s, and Paul's father, Jesse, began in 1968. Paul came on board in 1992.

Paul uses up to four bean threshers. His grandfather Albert began with a 1948 C.B. Hay thresher. Paul added a 1949 C.B. Hay he purchased from Jack Broome and a 1955 G.E. Price he bought from Larry Nunes in 2004. Recently, Paul purchased a 1986 C.B. Hay thresher, the most modern of the old-school separators.

Paul has planted and harvested up to three hundred acres each year for the last thirty-one years and counting. He has also threshed beans for Jim Gill and the Naumanns when needed. At one time, Paul harvested Fordhook seed for Pictsweet. In 1998, Paul was introduced to a variety of lima bean seeds by Jerry Sweetland. Sweetland owned Ventura County Seed Growers in downtown Oxnard at 127 West Third Street for over sixty years. He was instrumental in working with the State of Department of Agriculture, the California Crop Improvement Association, California Lima Bean Association and Ferry Morse Seed Company as early as the 1950s to produce purified seed. With an eye out for improved seeds, Sweetland introduced Paul and Jess DeBusschere to the Lee Large Lima bean. The Lee Lima Bean came out of UC Davis Foundation Seed Program. The seed is a combination of the Ventura seed and Mackie seed.

Mike Naumann began growing Fordhooks in 1996 for Dean Foods. By the year 2000, Mike was joined in his farming operations by his brother Brian. The brothers grew Fordhooks for several companies, including Pictsweet, Birds Eye, Coastal Growers and AgriLink. They also got back into the game of growing dry lima beans in 2008. By 2023, the brothers were planting 780 acres to dry limas.

The Naumann family presence in Ventura County reaches back to 1898. The Samuel Naumann family hailed from Aschersleben, Germany. Samuel was married to Rosina Christina Wilke, and they left Germany with their seven children in 1886. They arrived in Goliad County, Texas, near the town of Schroeder, where he soon learned he had been swindled by the man who offered to sponsor the family. Samuel rented land for a few years and by 1891 had purchased 104 acres for $10 an acre. He planted cotton and watermelons. By 1893, Samuel and Rosina had packed up their now eight children and took a train that landed them in Chino, California, where a sugar refinery was recently built by the Oxnard brothers. Samuel tried his hand at raising sugar beets. By 1898, the Oxnards had completed their

Mike Naumann coming up the wind row of cut and dry limas off Las Posas Road in the fall of 2023. *Jeff Maulhardt.*

second California factory in Ventura County and the Naumanns packed their bags one last time. After a few years of unsuccessfully growing beets on the marshier parts of the plain, Samuel learned of a parcel off Etting Road that gave the family a chance to grow beets and lima beans for a profit. He purchased the 159-acre parcel in 1901 for $14,000. By 1904, Samuel had added an adjoining 79.75 acres.

Soon, the sons of Samuel would be planting lima beans and threshing their beans as well as beans for the neighboring farmers. The Naumann brothers took on varying roles in the operation, with Gus acting as the general roustabout by hiring the men, handling the wages and buying supplies for the cookhouse. Paul Naumann was in charge of the stationary, one-cylinder gas generator, and Otto was in charge of the horses. Herman Naumann was in charge of the separator.

While the Naumann brothers continued to work in agriculture for many years, few lasted until the fifth generation. Descendants of Herman

Naumann Bros.
1909

The Naumann Brothers threshing outfit included brothers Gus, Herman, Otto and Paul. Descendants Mike, Brian and Joey Naumann carry on the bean tradition over one hundred years later. *Frank Naumann.*

Naumann stayed in the game. Herman was followed in the ranching business by his son Herbert, who was followed by sons James and Richard Naumann. James grew Fordhook lima beans for Oxnard Frozen Foods Cooperative. James was joined by his sons Mike and Brian. As of 2023, sixth-generation Naumann and son of Mike Naumann, Joey, has joined the lima bean team.

The Naumanns relied on four different machines, all C.B. Hay Big Bertha threshers, to get the job done. The oldest machine is a 1951 out of Lompoc, then a 1957 bought from the Jim Gill estate, a 1981 bought machine out of Santa Maria and a 1988 C.B. Hay from Salinas.

James Reiman, a cousin to Mike and Brian Naumann, as well as Paul Debusschere, is another fifth-generation farmer who also has deep roots in agriculture in Ventura County with no fewer than six relatives who farmed in Ventura County over a century ago. James's earliest ancestors to the area included Louis Pfeiler, who came in 1868 and Michael Kaufmann, who came the same year. His other farming ancestors include Joseph Reiman (1881), Jacob Seckinger (1889) Samuel Naumann (1898) and Hector DeBusschere (1909).

James and son Conner Reiman take a break in front of their thresher after threshing beans off Cawelti Road, fall 2023. *Jeff Maulhardt.*

In 2022, James, along with his son Conner, jumped back onto the lima bean field. His father, William, spent much of his farming career up a thresher. James joined forces with Rio Farms to begin growing and harvesting two hundred acres of lima beans. He uses a 1956 C.B. Hay Big Bertha machine that came from John Maring of Patterson. The Marings previously farmed in Oxnard.

At one time, Ventura County offered ten lima bean warehouses spread throughout the county: El Rio, Montalvo, Saticoy, Hueneme, Santa Paula, Moorpark, Camarillo, Somis, Oxnard and Pleasant Valley, between Oxnard and Camarillo. By 1972, only Saticoy and Pleasant Valley remained. Within two years, Saticoy closed, leaving Pleasant Valley as the last remaining warehouse. However, the one-and-a-half-story wood-frame building in Saticoy, constructed in 1917 and located at 10995 Azahar Street, was deemed a Ventura County Landmark in 1988.

By 1993, the Pleasant Valley Lima Bean Warehouse was down to fifteen employees during its final season in September of that year. The warehouse took in its last load of beans from Bill Lenox and Paul DeBusschere. The building would sit vacant for a few years before it was leased for strawberry distribution, and by 2012, it had become home to the Oxnard Pallet Company.

Locally grown beans would need to find a new home for processing, if anyone was willing to still grow lima beans. The end of an era looked imminent. Over one hundred years of farming lima beans in Ventura County was about to end. The one-time Lima Bean Capital of the World was about to be home of an abandoned crop.

To the rescue came Francis Giudici, from L.A. Hearne Company in King City. Francis believed the lima beans grown in Ventura County were the best in the world. Paul met with Francis, and the beans were resown in the county. For a while, from 2003 to 2008, Paul was the "Lone Ranger" growing beans. Paul pointed out, "Although it was nice to have a warehouse here, I cannot say enough good things about my experience with Francis and the whole Hearne family. Had it not been for them, I'd have quit the bean business years ago and Jim Gill and the Naumann brothers would probably not have joined with that relationship either. It has been a great ride."[53]

The remaining bean warehouse in California is located in King City and owned by the L.A. Hearne Company, a family-run business in King City since 1938. After managing a dry bean warehouse in San Joaquin Valley, Larry Hearne moved to King City and founded King City Warehouse Co., a bean cleaning operation. Hearne was also instrumental in reviving the planting of the pink bean, which went from fourteen thousand acres in Salinas Valley in 1940 to the point of abandonment ten years later due to disease troubles. Working with the agricultural extension services in Monterey County and the Salina Land Company, they came up with a new variety that would revive the planting of the pink bean.

One of Larry Hearne's innovations helped save time and money for the business. He convinced his growers to bring in their beans in bulk to be clean, sorted and bagged. He next came up with the "seeing eye" sorter, which automatically sorted the beans and eliminated the unwanted items such as rocks, dirt clods and bad beans.

Hearne changed the name of the business to L.A. Hearne Co. in 1960, and the company was incorporated. His four sons joined him in the business. Today the company is run by his eight grandchildren. While still in the business of conditioning and selling dry beans, the company had branched out to offer fertilizer blending, application and sales, grain merchandizing, bulk and sacked manufacturing of feed, wholesale distribution of feed, pet foods, trucking with a fleet of trucks and trailer diversity for hauling and two

Third-generation cousins of the Hearne family. *Left to right*: Jim Hearne, Mike Hearne, Francis Giudici, Tom Hearne, Brad Hearne, Matt Hearne, Steve Hearne and Peter Giudici. *Francis Giudici.*

retail farm stores. The company also owns two threshing machines available to plant and harvest several hundred acres of lima beans.

Francis Giudici is the sales and field operations manager for the company, and he is the one who communicates with the Ventura County farmers. He is part of the third generation of family running the company. In his opinion, the dry limas from Ventura County are not only the best in the state but the world as well. This is because of the favorable soil on the Oxnard Plain as well as the perfect climate for the growth of the beans and, finally, the skill of the remaining growers. Francis was also instrumental in sharing his insights of the industry.

Lima beans in King City have had a connection to Ventura County as far back as 1917 when Abe Hobson, John Lagomarsino, Charles Teague and Fred Smith formed the Salinas Land Company. The California Orchard Company was formed as a subsidy of the company to manage the fruit production, and Teague served as the president. They took over the 9,000 acres of the William Dunphy ranch, which included an addition 5,000 in grazing land for a total of 13,700 acres. The purchase price was $310,000.

The Salinas Company immediately began improving the property by sinking wells, adding irrigation, planting fruit trees and devoting nearly 1,600 acres to lima beans. Over time, the company would subdivide portions of the land while retaining a large percentage. The names of Hobson, Teague and Lagomarsino would all be honored with street signs off Route 101 between Salinas and King City.

Francis Giudici and the Hearne Company provide the Ventura County farmers with their lima bean seed. Benefiting from the delivery of beans is the Oxnard Historic Farm Park, which not only plants a demonstration garden of lima beans each year but also offers a two-pound bag of lima beans in a collectible burlap sack.

In addition, these same seeds grown on the Oxnard Plain by our local farmers are beginning to make a comeback in Ventura County restaurants, including Spanish Hills Club. The restaurant's recipe for Chef Ken's lima bean hummus is located in the recipe chapter. Another recipe from the Camarillo restaurant Adolfo Grill, ranchero chili with lima beans, is printed in the final chapter.

Stacked inside the Hearne Co warehouse are eighteen totes of four thousand pounds, two tons of lima beans earmarked for Great Britain and Italy. *Jeff Maulhardt* .

Lima beans are grown in a demonstration plot at the Oxnard Historic Farm Park every year by the Master Gardeners of Ventura County led by Terry Ball. The beans are planted along with the county's other early crops of barley, corn and sugar beets. *Jeff Maulhardt.*

Also, the Oxnard Historic Farm Park will be offering an annual Lima Bean Fest on the second Saturday of September beginning in 2024. While Ventura County used to offer many Lima Bean Festivals in the past, it's been over fifty years since the last one in Camarillo. The only other Lima Bean Festival in the country is in New Jersey, in the city of Cape May. However, the Lima Bean Fest in Oxnard will feature a lima bean tasting contest, a lima bean thresher display and demonstration, a slide show of lima beans over the years, lima bean guessing games, lima bean recipes, lima beans for sale and, of course, this book, *Ventura County Lima Beans: A History*, with more books on the subject to follow.

In conclusion, we've learned about the importance of lima beans to the development of and contributions to Ventura County. We have learned about the many nutritional benefits and the new recognition of its value as a superfood.

Finally, we've learned that lima beans could be a key to being a climate resilient crop from results of a four-year research project out of the University of California, Davis. The experiments span several institutions, including Delaware Valley University and Plowshare Farms in Pipersville, Pennsylvania. The early conclusions are that lima beans are a "climate smart crop." The wild lima bean, naturally grown in Central and South America, can adapt to grow in hotter, drier, wetter, colder and more stressful climates that the common bean. Another advantage is the lima beans are nitrogen fixing and can build their own plant food as well as being a good rotation crop. The only thing left to improve the fate of the lima bean is to find the right recipe.

With all this good news, it's no wonder that lima beans are on the rebound. We were the Lima Bean Capital of the World, and we haven't given up!

7

LIMA BEAN RECIPES

As mentioned in the introduction of this book, regarding the popularity of lima beans, people either love them or hate them. One reason some people disliked the beans in the past is because of either the way they were cooked or because of the type of bean used. As Jim Munson, manager of the California Dry Bean Advisory Board, pointed out in a 1997 article in the *Ventura County Star*, most people grew up eating the smaller, green canned or frozen beans and therefore did not get the full flavor the bean has to offer. "When large limas are dried then cooked, they rehydrate and they're much softer and I think more flavorful."

Humans are not the only bean consumers: some felines like the limas. Tommy the cat was not a finicky eater when it came to the cooked bean. His owner, Thomas Hollida, worked at Oxnard Frozen Foods as a security officer and would often bring home the beans without the bacon. Hollida claimed the cat wouldn't eat meat or drink milk but would scarf down limas every day. He also claimed his cat was a very healthy cat because the beans were high in protein, carbohydrates, iron and vitamins.

Today, the lima bean is recognized as a superfood. Its macronutrients consist of high levels of protein, fiber and iron, the building blocks for muscle growth, oxygenation and blood sugar regulation. One cup of lima beans contains roughly one-quarter of the daily recommended amount of iron. Other micronutrients include thiamine, molybdenum, folate, potassium, phosphorus, zinc and vitamin C. The manganese acts an antioxidant. The copper supports immune health and promotes brain function. All these nutrients contribute to the increased processing of carbohydrates, activating enzymes, helping prevent cardiovascular disease and promoting the formation of bones and teeth.[54]

Lima beans also help control diabetes. Legumes are low-glycemic food and rich in soluble fiber, which helps the body absorb carbohydrates and regulate blood sugar levels. Because the beans are high in fiber, they can also aid in weight control by making you feel full longer. In addition, the beans aid the digestion of insoluble fiber, or roughage. And another advantage of lima beans is that they are the only fat-free legume.[55]

There's no cholesterol or trans fats, suggesting the beans help lower LDL, or "bad," cholesterol. They even also help prevent anemia, though those taking anemia medication would be cautioned to check with their doctors.[56] Also, those taking anti-psychotic medication are advised to check with their physicians.

However, not all news is good news with the limas. The roots and leaves of lima beans contain linamarin, which when ingested, breaks down into hydrogen cyanide. Raw and uncooked lima beans contain three thousand milligrams of linamarin per kilogram. Two pounds of raw, uncooked beans can kill twenty people, meaning it takes only a few beans to kill a person. However, once limas are cooked for ten minutes, the threat is gone. Today, the bean grown in the United States contains a little over one hundred milligrams of linamarin per kilogram.

Talk of creating a flour out of lima bean dates back as early as 1909. An article in the *Morning Press* under the title "First Recipes for Lima Beans" written by W.A. Carney pointed out that if lima beans were made into flour and sold as the prepared bread or as prepared pumpkin was being sold, lima bean flour would become a large part of the market.

Lima Bean Croquettes

1 pint cold lima beans
Salt and pepper
2 eggs, beaten
Bread crumbs
Tomato sauce
2 tablespoons cream
2 slices onion
4 cloves

Mash lima beans, season with salt and pepper and work in 1 well-beaten egg. Form into croquettes; roll in beaten egg and then in bread crumbs and fry in deep fat to a golden brown. Boil tomato sauce with cream, onions and cloves and pour over croquettes.

A FEW YEARS LATER, in 1912, a man named Andy Ruthrauff was in town from Newton, Kansas, to visit his brother-in-law A.C. Vickers. Ruthrauff was an expert mill man and proposed making some special machinery to grind the beans into a fine powder. Others had produced similar flour in small quantities, but the cost of building a complete mill was cost-prohibitive. Ruthrauff either dropped the ball or dropped the lima beans because nothing more was written about his efforts.

During tough times, lima beans served as an alternative to beef as a protein source. During World War I, the *Progressive Farmer* magazine published a substitute for meatloaf in March 1918.

Potato and Lima Bean Loaf

1 ⅓ cups cooked lima beans (sieved)
2 tablespoons fat
¼ cup milk
1 teaspoon salt
⅓ teaspoon sage
2 cups riced potato

½ teaspoon fat
½ teaspoon fat for brushing

Mix the first five ingredients and place in bottom of oiled dish. Whip together the hot potato and remaining ingredients. Place this mixture on top. Bake in quick oven. Serve with tomato sauce.

Bean Loaf
This 1920 recipe offers up another substitute for meat loaf.

2 cups cooked beans
1 cup cooked rice
1 cup bread crumbs
1 egg
1 tablespoon fat
½ tablespoon salt
⅛ teaspoon paprika

Put beans through sieve or grind in a meat grinder. Mix all ingredients well. Form into a loaf and bake until brown. Baste frequently with amounts of liquid containing a tablespoon of fat to a cup of hot water.

A DECADE AFTER RUTHRAUFF'S efforts, progress was made on developing a lima bean flour. In 1922, Dr. William D. Sansum, a physician and dietitian from Santa Barbara, became the first physician to develop and administer insulin to treat a diabetic patient. He was also instrumental in making orange juice a national health drink. In 1927, he began experimenting with developing a flour to be used for making bread. It was being predicted that the flour made from the lima beans could be used to make bread with many health benefits. The lima bean was long recognized for its high alkaline content. The ills corrected by the bean flower included acidosis, high blood pressure and hardening of the arteries. In March 1927, the Joseph Powers Company announced the sale of lima bean flour. It sold the flour at fifteen cents a pound in five- and one-hundred-pound sacks. But producing the flour was costly.

Ralph L. Churchill, the manager of the California Lima Bean Association, found a mill in Alhambra to produce the flour according to Dr. Sansum's specifications and approved by the Priscilla Proving Plant, a company out of Boston that tested recipes. Soon after, the California Lima Bean Growers Association began advertising the sale of the flour. But the high price of production and low gluten content made the flour hard to bake with.

The *Ventura County Star* made a public plea on April 23, 1927. Addressed to Bill Baker, the column read: "Dear Bill: I'm wondering whether Ventura County cannot be made nationally famous in the next five years as the home of lima bean flour, lima bean bread, lima bean cookies and lima bean delicacies of many sorts not yet dreamed of. I'm wondering if you couldn't be instrumental in launching the industry on a big scale."

The message got to the baker, and he proved to be a fortune teller. W.C. Bill Baker was a noted baker from Ojai, and he came up with a mixture that proved flavorful and easier to bake with. Baker sent a loaf of his lima bean bread to the American Institute of Baking in Chicago, where it was

In 1927, Bill Baker from Ojai came up with lima bean flour. Baker also helped promote Ventura County by sending several presidents ceremonial cakes. *Museum of Ventura County, photograph 11710-85.*

tested and found to meet the requirement for a health food. The favorable results were published in the *Journal of the American Bakers Association* on February 15, 1928.

Bill Baker continued experimenting with the lima bean flower and came up with a lima bean wafer. He added a new building next to his original bakery, with the new build dedicated to producing lima bean products. By the next year, 1930, it was predicted that the success of Baker's flour would increase the valuation of nearly $1 million annually on the Orange County crop of limas.[57]

It should be noted that Bill Baker was also famous for baking elaborately decorated cakes that he sent to several U.S. presidents. In 1929, Baker sent a fifty-pound Christmas fruit cake to President Herbert Hoover. In 1934, Baker created the world's largest cake with a one-ton birthday cake for the Los Angeles school system to feed an audience of 100,000 people. The cake was twenty-one feet in circumference and seven feet in diameter with two hundred roses, one thousand birds and a replica of a little red schoolhouse. In 1935, Baker sent a one-hundred-pound fruit cake to President Franklin Roosevelt, and a few years later, he sent Roosevelt a second cake with a replica of the Golden Gate Bridge.

In 1939, Baker created one of his most extravagant cakes for the Golden Gate Exposition at San Francisco. The eight-hundred-pound cake also included sixty pounds of sugar, sixty pounds of butter, fifty dozen eggs, fifteen pounds of honey, fifty pounds of walnuts, fifty pounds of pecans, seventy-five pounds of cherries, thirty pounds of figs, two hundred pounds of raisins, ten gallons of California wine and five pounds of mixed spices. The cake featured three tiers and included an octagonal bottom with the nineteen California missions.

As early as 1920, the Lima Bean Growers Association began advertise lima bean recipes in several national magazines and newspapers. Among the recipes were lima bean croquette, lima bean soufflé, lima bean salad, lima bean chowder and lima bean puree.

The Lima Bean Growers Association put out a thirty-two-page pamphlet in 1932 titled *How Ten Editors Serve California Limas*. The contributors ranged from Good Housekeeping Institute to a recipe by Sarah Field Splint, the director of the food department or *McCall's Magazine*. The categories included recipes for main course dishes, salad recipes, soup recipes and a few words on why California limas were of the highest quality.

The basic recipe for cooking limas includes soaking the dried limas in cold water for 6 to 8 hours. Drain. Cover with boiling water and cook slowly for 30 minutes. Add salt after 20 minutes of cooking.

One of the more interesting offerings is poverty stew. Given that the country was in the midst of a decadelong economic depression, ways to save money and feed a hungry family were truly welcome.

The California Lima Bean Growers Association and later the women's charity group the Forty Leaguers put out several small pamphlets that not only listed a variety of recipes but also included tips on how to cook the beans as well as their nutritional value. *Julia Ann Maulhardt.*

Poverty Stew
2 cups cooked dried limas
1 onion
½ teaspoon salt
⅛ teaspoon paprika
¼ teaspoon mustard
1 cup diced salt pork
1 cup milk

Mix ingredients and turn into a buttered baking dish and bake 1 hour in a moderate oven (300 degrees).

Succotash
1 cup cooked dried limas
2 cups corn
½ teaspoon salt
½ teaspoon sugar
⅛ teaspoon pepper
1 tablespoon butter
¾ cup cream

Combine ingredients and heat in a double boiler over hot water.

Other advertised dishes included creamed limas, limas with bacon, limas with mock hollandaise, tamale pie, lima soufflé, limas creole, chile limas, limas en casserole, lima and walnut salad and Limas California, which included two hard-cooked eggs and a tablespoon of lemon juice.

Several local eateries became known for their tasty lima bean offerings, including the Sportsman in Ventura and Judy's Sandwich shop in Camarillo. Judy's became known for its lima bean soup as early as 1946. The shop was run by Hyman Polonsky and his wife, Irene. They named the shop after their daughter. Irene came up with the recipe, and "Hy" focused on hand peeling each bean before "crushing the beans to bits." Next, onions, pepper, garlic and seasoning were added and cooked. A few whole beans were dropped in for good measure. It was said that "the lima bean soup makes your palate and taste buds drunk with ecstasy."[58]

The ten-stool counter restaurant averaged 7,500 bowls per year and 500 gallons of lima bean soup. Unfortunately, Judy's Sandwich Shop was one of ninety building that had to be moved for the construction of the 101 Highway expansion in 1952.

The California Farm Bureau Federation held a lima bean recipe contest in 1956, and the first prize went to Miss Irene Maitre from La Habra, California, for her lima bean and beef-ball casserole.

Lima Bean and Beef-Ball Casserole

1 (10-ounce) package frozen lima beans
2–3 slices bread
1 ½ cups milk
1 ½ teaspoons salt
½ teaspoon pepper
1 egg
1 clove garlic
1 pound ground beef
4 tablespoons butter
1 ½ cups water
1 cup sour cream
Paprika for garnish

Start oven at 350 F. Cook lima beans until tender. Drain. Soak slices of bread in milk. In a separate bowl, mix salt, pepper, egg, grated garlic. Mix bread, ground beef and egg mixture into little balls. Fry in butter until brown and transfer to bottom of casserole; pour water into a skillet and stir; pour over meat balls. Season lima beans and add to meat in casserole. Bake 30 minutes. Add sour cream and cook five minutes. Sprinkle paprika. Serves 4.

THE FORTY LEAGUERS OF Ventura County put out a recipe compilation in 1976 titled *Lemons, Limas and Leaguers*. The philanthropic group was organized in October 1938, with Artie Duval acting as the inaugural president. Among the lima bean offerings that came from the original Forty Leaguers cookbooks was this one by Emily Wucherpfennig.

Addie's Lima Bean Soup

2 cups dried lima beans
4 slices bacon, diced
1 medium onion, diced
3 cups water
2 teaspoons catsup
Salt and pepper
2 heaping spoonfuls sour cream

Boil beans 10 minutes. Rinse in cold water and discard skins. Fry bacon and add onion. Add bacon fat to skinned limas. Add 3 cups of water and catsup. Bring to boil. Reduce heat to low. Cook one hour. Add salt and pepper. Sour cream added before serving. Flavors improve with reheating. Serves 4 to 5.

California Barbecued Lima Beans
Another recipe from the original Forty Leaguers cookbook by Barbara McDivitt.

1 pound dry limas
4 slices bacon, diced
1 large onion, chopped
2 cloves garlic, minced
3 stalks celery, chopped
1 green pepper, chopped
3 tablespoons bacon drippings
Salt and pepper
Dash oregano
2 (8-ounce) cans tomato sauce

3 tablespoons mild vinegar
2 tablespoons prepared mustard
2 tablespoons Worcestershire sauce
1 teaspoon brown sugar
Chili powder to taste
Few drops of liquid smoke

Soak limas in water overnight. Drain and add fresh water and bacon. Simmer until nearly done and drain and save bean liquid. Sauté onion, garlic, celery and pepper in bacon drippings. Add remaining ingredients and pour over limas in a pot or casserole. Add enough bean liquid to make soupy consistency. Bake 350 for 1 hour. Good with barbecue chicken and baked ham, served with green salad.

Do-Ahead Ham and Bean Soup
A third recipe from the Forty Leaguers recipe book from Roxann Tobias

1 ½ cups large dry lima beans
1 quart water
1 meaty ham bone (1 pound)
1 cup chopped onion
½ teaspoon salt
½ teaspoon dried marjoram, crushed
Dash pepper
1 (16-ounce) can mixed vegetables
1 cup water

In large saucepan, cover beans with 1 quart of water and bring to a boil. Simmer 2 minutes. Remove from heat and let stand 1 hour. Do not drain. Add ham bone, onion, salt, marjoram and pepper. Cover and simmer until tender (1 ½ hours). Remove ham bone. Cut up ham and discard bone. With potato masher, mash limas slightly. Add ham, un-drained mixed vegetables and 1 cup of water to soup. Heat through. Serves 6–8.

Cowboy Beans

The Women of the Moose, Chapter #1957, Camarillo, put out a recipe book in 1992, featuring these Cowboy Beans by Melodie Kelly.

½ pound ground beef
1 whole onion
1 cup yellow butter beans
1 cup pinto beans
1 cup baked beans
1 cup brown sugar
1 small bottle of catsup
1 tablespoon hickory smoke
1 tablespoon vinegar
1 ½ ounces bacon bits
Salt to taste

Bring to a simmer and keep low 2 hours.

Lima Beans 'n Pretzels

2 packages frozen limas
1 can cream of mushroom soup
½ cup milk
1 small can chopped mushrooms
1 jar pimientos, chopped
1 cup crushed pretzels

Cook lima beans as directed. Mix soup and milk together. Add all ingredients except pretzels to drained lima beans. Pour into greased casserole. Cover with pretzels. Heat for 30 minutes at 350.

Lima Beans with Marshmallows

If lima beans can be made with pretzels, how about lima beans with marshmallows? From a one-hundred-year-old recipe:

1 pound dry lima beans
3 tablespoons butter
3 tablespoons brown sugar
Salt and pepper
4 strips bacon
1 dozen marshmallows

Soak lima beans in cold water for five hours. Drain off water and add boiling water to cover. Cook on a low flame for half an hour. Melt butter and add sugar and seasoning. Add beans to a greased casserole dish, pour over butter and seasoning. Lay strips of bacon on top. Bake with cover on for one hour at 350 degree. Add water if necessary. Remove cover and put marshmallows on top of bacon. Brown under a broiler.

Tacos American

A recipe from the *Thousand Oaks Star*, August 15, 1873

2 tablespoons butter
6 frankfurters, chopped
1 package taco seasoning
1 can tomato sauce
¼ cup chopped dill pickle
2 cups coarsely cut lettuce
¼ cup chopped onion
12 taco shells or 12 tortillas
2 cups shredded cheddar cheese

In a large skillet, melt butter and brown frankfurters. Stir in seasoning, tomato sauce and pickle. Bring to boil, then reduce heat and simmer for 15 minutes. In a medium bowl, toss together lettuce and onion. Fill shells with meat, then lettuce and top with cheese.

SPAM 3-Bean Casserole
From frankfurters to SPAM

1 cup SPAM
1 package frozen lima beans
1 cup baked beans
1 can kidney beans
1 can tomato sauce
2 tablespoons chili sauce
1 small onion
2 tablespoons brown sugar
1 teaspoon salt
¼ teaspoon dry mustard

Cut SPAM into 8 slices. Partially cook lima beans. Drain and mix with baked beans and kidney beans. Combine tomato sauce, chili sauce, onion, brown sugar, salt and dry mustard. Add to beans. Pour into a 1½-quart round casserole. Arrange SPAM slices in spoke fashion on top. Bake at 400 for 30 minutes. 4 to 6 servings.

Limas Con Chiles Con Queso

1 pound large, dry limas
¼ teaspoon basil or thyme
⅛ teaspoon oregano
2 (4-ounce) cans whole mild green chiles
6–8 ounces Jack or sharp Cheddar cheese
¾ cup sour cream

Cook limas. Drain while hot, save liquid. Spread ⅓ of the limas in a 2½-quart casserole dish. Sprinkle with half of each herb. Tear chiles lengthwise, cut crosswise in half-inch-wide strips. Scatter half the chiles and a third of cheese over layer of beans. Repeat layers. Top with beans and sprinkle with cheese. Stir bean liquid into sour cream, mix smooth. Add salt if needed and pour over casserole. Bake uncovered at 325 degrees for 30–45 minutes. Serves 8–10.

Seabreeze Lima Beans

Winner of the Ventura County Fair's first Casserole Contest in 1985 was Anne Stewart from Simi Valley.

3 ham hocks
3 bay leaves
1 onion, finely chopped
1 pound lima beans, parboiled
1 cup chopped tomato (drain if using canned)
1 teaspoon oregano
Salt and pepper
Monosodium glutamate

Simmer ham and bay leaves in water for 3 hours to produce 3 cups of stock. Sauté onion. Take 2 cups of stock, lima beans, sautéed onion and tomato; add oregano, salt and pepper to taste and dash of monosodium glutamate; incorporate ham hock meat, chopped. Discard fat, skin and bones of ham hocks. De-grease stock. Place ingredients in casserole and bake at 375 degrees for one hour. Garnish with parsley.

RECENT RECIPES

Francis's Savory Large Limas (Butter Beans)

Francis Giudici is the sales and field management officer for the Hearne Company, and he has come up with a recipe his office staff especially likes.

¾ pound lean chorizo
3 pound dry large limas (about 6 cups)
2–3 white or yellow onions, chopped
6 cloves garlic, minced
1 red bell pepper, chopped
1 (28-ounce) can crushed tomatoes
16 ounces tomatillo (green) salsa
11 ounces canned green chilies
2 smoked ham hocks or 1.2 pounds chopped bacon
1 tablespoons honey
32 ounces beef, chicken or vegetable broth
Sage and thyme

Cook chorizo until brown and spoon out grease. Rinse beans—do not soak—set aside. Simmer onions and garlic—simmer until tender. Add peppers, tomatoes, tomatillo, chilies, ham hocks/bacon and honey. Add stock. Season with sage and thyme to taste. Bring to a slow boil—about 35 minutes—with lid cracked. Add beans and stir occasionally. Add water/stock to level above beans, as they will expand. Slowly boil for 2.5–3 hours; stir occasionally. Remove bones from hocks. Slightly salt and pepper. After cooking, keep lid cracked to allow beans to breath.

Ranchero Chili with Lima Beans—Adolfo Grill

5 pounds 80/20 ground beef
2 tablespoons paprika
2 tablespoons granulated garlic
2 tablespoons granulated onion
2 tablespoons salt
2 tablespoons black pepper
1 tablespoons red chili flakes
3 fresh jalapeño, diced
2 yellow onions, diced
2 pasillas chilis, diced
2 red bell peppers, diced
1½ pounds cooked lima beans
30 ounces tomato sauce
20 ounces whole peeled tomatoes

Day before, rinse and drain lima beans, cover with water and soak overnight. Day of, drain soaked beans, cover with fresh water and bring to a boil; simmer beans for 1½ hours until tender. Drain and set aside.

In large pot, brown ground beef, breaking it up with wooden spoon. Drain fat.

Add all dried spices, stir well. Add diced peppers, peppers and onions, tomato sauce and whole tomatoes. Simmer 1 hour. Stir in cooked lima beans 5 minutes before serving.

Optional topping for chili: cheddar cheese, green onions, sour cream, avocado.

Chef Ken's Lima Bean Hummus—Spanish Hills Club

3 cups lima beans
Bay leaf to cook beans
¼ cup tahini
¼ cup bean cooking liquid
2 cloves garlic
2 tablespoons extra virgin olive oil
1 tablespoon lemon juice
1 tablespoon lime juice
2 teaspoons kosher salt
White ground pepper to taste
Paprika to taste
1 teaspoon red chili pepper flakes
1 teaspoon chives
½ teaspoon crunchy sea salt

Rinse beans under running water. Soak for 4–5 hours. Pour soaked beans with liquid into a pot with liquid; cover beans at least 3 inches. Over medium heat, bring beans to a rolling boil and boil for 10–15 minutes. Turn pot down to medium and simmer for 2 hours until beans are soft.

Hummus is best if beans are blended while hot. For food processor, place towel over opening of lid while blending. In blender or food processor, add all ingredients except cooking liquid and blend, starting on lowest setting and working up to high speed. Periodically stop blender to scrape sides and continue blending. Slowing pour liquid into mix for desired consistency. Garnish with sea salt, chives and chili pepper flakes. Serve hummus with raw veggies, pita chips or crackers.

Deb's Lima Bean Trinity

1 pound dry lima beans, rinsed
4 tablespoons unsalted butter
The Trinity: 1 cup chopped white onions; 1 cup chopped green peppers; 1 cup chopped celery
3 garlic cloves minced
5–6 cups chicken broth
1 smoked turkey leg or 1 ham hock
1 bay leaf
Garnish with ketchup or Creole seasoning.

Wash beans and cover with 4 inches of water. Bring to a boil. Soak for 15 minutes; then drain and rinse beans. Place large soup pot on medium heat and add butter. Add Trinity and garlic. Sauté until fragrant. Add chicken broth, lima beans, smoked turkey or ham and bay leaf. Stir. Place lid on pot and lower heat to medium-low. Cook around 2 hours, until beans are soft. Open pot and remove bay leaf and meat. Shred meat, discarding bone, and return to the pot. Cool before serving. Garnish with ketchup or Creole seasoning and enjoy with some cornbread! The author likes to have his beans with a grilled cheese sandwich.

Modern recipes and methods of cooking can be found on the website www.calbeans.org. In addition to storage methods, the site offers soaking and cooking methods as well as Marilyn's Kitchen tips. It makes sense to end the chapter and the book on a dessert recipe from the site. This recipe uses "white beans" which is in reference to a group of legumes with white castings and starchy insides, and they include navy beans, cannellini beans, great northern beans and lima beans.

White Bean Ginger Chew

¼ cup butter
½ cup granulated sugar
½ cup cooked white beans
1 tablespoon molasses
¼ cup flour
2 teaspoons ground ginger
1 teaspoon ground cinnamon
¼ teaspoon baking soda
1 pinch salt
1 large white egg white

Melt butter in medium saucepan and let cool. Pour butter into bowl of food processor; add sugar and beans and process until smooth. Pour contents back into unwashed saucepan and cook over medium heat until mixture boils. Remove pan from heat, stir in molasses and allow to cool for 20 minutes.

Preheat oven 325 degrees. In a small bowl, stir together the flour, ginger, cinnamon, baking soda and salt. Once sugar and bean mixture cools, add egg white. Add flour mixture to the pot and stir in. Drop by teaspoonfuls onto baking sheets that have been sprayed with nonstick spray. Bake 10–12 minutes.

NOTES

1. A Ship from Lima

1. *Oxnard Courier*, December 24, 1915.
2. "A History of Lima Beans," *Carpinteria Herald*, May 2, 1967.
3. Sheridan, *History of Ventura County*, vol. 2.
4. "History of Lima Beans."
5. *Morning Press*, December 27, 1872.
6. *Santa Barbara Weekly Press*, July 17, 1875.
7. *Ventura Signal*, January 31, 1880.

2. From Barley to Limas

8. *Ventura County Star*, June 24, 1927.
9. *San Francisco Examiner*, July 12, 1889.
10. WikiTree, "George Gregg Briggs," https://www.wikitree.com/wiki/Briggs-624.
11. *Ventura County Historical Society Quarterly* 8, no. 2 (February 1963).
12. *Ventura County Historical Society Quarterly* 3, no. 1 (November 1957).
13. Ibid.
14. *Ventura Signal*, January 18, 1879.

15. *Ventura County Historical Society Quarterly* 1, no. 2 (February 1956).
16. *Ventura Weekly Post and Democrat*, September 26, 1889.
17. *Ventura Signal*, May 2, 1872.
18. *Ventura County Historical Society Quarterly* 20, no. 3 (Spring 1975).
19. *Ventura County Historical Society Quarterly: The Garden of the World* 46, Whole Year Issue 2002.
20. *Ventura County Star*, July 23, 1927.
21. *Ventura Free Press*, May 4, 1878.

3. Limas Come to Ventura County

22. Coastal View, January 21, 2021, https://www.coastalview.com.
23. *Ventura Signal*, April 17, 1875.
24. *Ventura County Historical Society Quarterly* 2, no. 1 (November 1956).
25. Bank of A Levy, *A Levy, A History*, 21.
26. Ibid.
27. Sheridan, *History of Ventura County*, 1:368.
28. *Ventura Weekly Post and Democrat*, September 26, 1889.
29. *Ventura Weekly Post and Democrat*, November 29, 1890.
30. *Ventura Free Press*, August 22, 1890.
31. *Ventura Free Press*, December 27, 1895.
32. Bank of A Levy, *A Levy, A History*, 47.
33. *Ventura Free Press*, November 20, 1896.
34. *Ventura Weekly Post and Democrat*, March 5, 1897.
35. *Oxnard Courier*, August 19, 1910.
36. *Ventura Free Press*, March 28, 1913.
37. *Oxnard Courier*, December 15, 1915.
38. *Oxnard Courier*, January 4, 1918.
39. *Ventura County Star*, January 8, 1941.
40. Jack Broome, taped interview by Jeff Maulhardt, July 2003.

4. The Threshers

41. *Ventura Weekly Post and Democrat*.
42. Ibid.

43. *Morning Free Press*, July 5, 1907.
44. *Ventura Weekly Post and Democrat*, September 23, 1892.
45. *Ventura Weekly Post and Democrat*, September 18, 1896.
46. *Sacramento Bee*, October 8, 1938.
47. *Ventura County Star*, October 20, 1953.
48. Craig Underwood, email interview, April 14, 2024.

5. The Workers

49. *Ventura Free Press*, March 23, 1894.
50. Godfrey, *Growing Up in Ventura County*.
51. *Camarillo Star*, August 21, 1931.
52. *Ventura County Star*, August 30, 1966.

6. Lima Beans Today

53. Paul Debusschere, text message to Jeffrey Maulhardt, December 12, 2023.

7. Lima Bean Recipes

54. T.C. Gunter, "Are Lima Beans Interesting? Actually, Yes," Medium, November 14, 2020, www.medium.com.
55. MDPI, "A Review of the Potential Food Application of Lima Beans," 2023, www.mdpi.com.
56. WebMD, "Health Benefits of Lima Beans," www.webmd.com.
57. *Morning Free Press*, January 15, 1930.
58. *Ventura County Star*, January 23, 1950.

BIBLIOGRAPHY

Newspapers

Camarillo Star
Carpinteria Herald
Morning Free Press
Morning Press
Oxnard Courier
Oxnard Daily Courier
Oxnard Press-Courier
Sacramento Bee
San Francisco Examiner
Santa Barbara Weekly Press
Ventura County Star
Ventura County Star–Free Press
Ventura Free Press
Ventura Signal
Ventura Weekly Post and Democrat

Article and Books

Bank of A Levy. *A Levy, A History.* Virginia Beach, VA: Donning Company, 1991.

Chess, Betsy Blanchard. *Daughter of the Land: Growing Up in the Citrus Capital of the Word: A Memoir.* Self-published, 2021.

A Comprehensive Story of Ventura County, California. Oxnard, CA: M&N Printing, 1979.

Gidney, C.M., Benjamin Brooks and Edwin Sheridan. *History of Santa Barbara, San Luis Obispo and Ventura Counties.* Chicago: Lewis Publishing, 1917.

Godfrey, Katherine McLoughlin. *Growing Up in Ventura County.* Self-published, 1990.

Naumann, Robert. *Ocean View Odyssey: The Life History of Robert G. Naumann.* Oxnard, CA: Robert Naumann, 1995.

Sheridan, Sol N. *History of Ventura County, California.* Vol. 2. Chicago: S.J. Clarke Publishing, 1926.

Storke, Yda Addis. *A Memorial and Biographical History of the Counties Santa Barbara, San Luis Obispo, and Ventura, California—Illustrated.* Chicago: Lewis Publishing, 1891.

Thompson, Thomas, and Albert West. *History of Santa Barbara & Ventura Counties, California with Illustrations,* Oakland, CA: Thompson & West, 1883.

Ventura County Historical Society Quarterly, various editions

ABOUT THE AUTHOR

Jeffrey Wayne Maulhardt is a fifth-generation descendant of two of the earliest farming families of Ventura County, Johannes Borchard and Jacob Maulhardt. Jeff taught history in the Oxnard School District and retired early to devote more time to serving as the director and founder of the Oxnard Historic Farm Park. He has authored seventeen local history books. This latest book on the history of lima beans is creating a lot of buzz in the community, as the popularity of lima beans has been rekindled with the limas once again making their way to the stoves of Ventura County.

Visit us at
www.historypress.com